KT-872-708

UNLOCKING NUMERACY

A Guide for Primary Schools

Edited by

Valsa Koshy
and Jean Murray

David Fulton Publishers
London

David Fulton Publishers Ltd
The Chiswick Centre, 414 Chiswick High Road, London W4 5TF

www. fultonpublishers.co.uk

First published in Great Britain by David Fulton Publishers 2002

Copyright © Valsa Koshy and Jean Murray 2002

British Cataloguing in Publication Data
A catalogue record for this book is available from the British Library.

ISBN 1–85346–835–5

All rights reserved. No part of this publication may be reproduced, stored in a retrieval system or transmitted, in any form, or by any means, electronic, mechanical, photocopying, recording or otherwise, without the prior permission of the publishers.

Typeset by Ann Buchan (Typesetters), Shepperton, Middlesex
Printed and bound in Great Britain by The Cromwell Press, Trowbridge, Wilts.

UNLOCKING NUMERACY

Contents

Acknowledgements

We would like to thank the many children, student teachers and teachers whose work has informed the contents of this book.

This book represents the collective endeavours of Brunel University's Mathematics Education Team over a number of years. We would like to express our gratitude to our past colleagues, Jan Potworoski and Christine Mitchell, for the support and inspiration they gave the team during their time working with us.

Notes on Contributors

Ron Casey is a Senior Research Fellow of the Brunel Able Children's Education (BACE) Centre at Brunel University. Development projects he is currently involved in include devising models of mathematical provision for able mathematicians and writing materials for mathematics enrichment for primary school pupils. His subject expertise is in mathematics and science.

Rachel Fairclough has taught mathematics within several 11–18 comprehensive schools, based in Essex, Oxfordshire and Surrey, where she was Head of Mathematics for four years. More recently she worked in a private school in Richmond, where she was Head of Faculty (science, mathematics and ICT) for two years. She has been a Key Stage 3 numeracy consultant in Hackney and still continues her role as numeracy consultant for Local Education Authorities on the west side of London, in particular Harrow. She joined Brunel University as a course tutor in mathematics in the School of Education with specific responsibility for secondary postgraduate Initial Teacher Training. Her current work includes the development of modular distance learning materials.

John Garvey taught for nine years in primary classrooms in London, and was the head teacher of a primary school in Richmond upon Thames. He now teaches in the Brunel School of Education across primary ITT courses with specialisms in Design and Technology and Information and Communication Technology. He is currently award leader for the PGCE primary course. His research interests include the use of databases and ICT to promote higher level thinking in mathematics. He is the author (with Robert Fisher) of *Investigating Technology* (Simon and Schuster).

Mark Humble taught mathematics in secondary schools for 13 years, holding a number of posts including head of department. He then held an advisory post for mathematics with a London LEA. He is now the Head of Mathematics in the School of Education at Brunel University, where he teaches on both primary and secondary courses for intending mathematics teachers. He is the Chair of Governors at a West London primary school. He has also undertaken extensive consultancy work in mathematics for Local Education Authorities. His research interests include the processes of mathematical problem solving and numeracy in the later years of schooling.

Bob Jeffery is a senior lecturer at Brunel University and former leader of the Mathematics Education team there. Before entering Higher Education he worked in secondary schools for a number of years. He is a former Chair of the Association of Mathematics Teachers, and has undertaken consultancy work in mathematics for a large number of Local Education Authorities and Higher Education Institutes. He has published extensively in the area of mathematics education, and has recently been working on the development of education policy and practice in Central Europe.

Valsa Koshy is Reader in Education at Brunel University. Prior to joining the University she was an advisory teacher for mathematics. She coordinates the mathematics in-service programme at the University and teaches mathematics to Initial Training students. She has published a number of practical books on the teaching of mathematics, some of which are included in the reference section at the end of her chapter.

Jean Murray taught for nine years in primary schools in Inner London. She now teaches on mathematics education and General Professional Studies courses in the School of Education at Brunel University. She has also undertaken consultancy work both nationally and internationally in mathematics education and in the development of the general primary curriculum. Her research interests include mental mathematics and low attainers in numeracy. She has published in a number of books and journals on primary mathematics issues.

Debbie Robinson has worked in education for over 20 years as a classroom teacher, advisory teacher and teacher trainer. Her work involved research on both the Graded Assessments in Mathematics and TVEI and Mathematics Projects. She is currently employed as a part-time lecturer at Brunel University and as a mathematics consultant for Beam Education, having recently co-written the book *Teaching Mental Strategies*.

Introduction

The last three years have witnessed the introduction of some major initiatives in the teaching of mathematics in England and Wales. As a result of the concerns raised by Ofsted reports over a number of years and the relatively low ranking of British children in international comparisons, a National Numeracy Strategy (DfEE 1998) was implemented. A National Numeracy Task Force was appointed and, on the basis of the recommendations made by the members of this group, a Framework for Teaching Mathematics (DfEE 1999) was issued to all primary schools. Evidence suggests that the Numeracy Framework has been welcomed by most teachers. In this context, it has been interesting to note that one of the questions often raised by teachers is: *What do we mean by 'numeracy'? Does it mean mathematics or do we mean working with aspects of number only?*

The definition given to 'numeracy' by the National Numeracy Framework (DfEE 1998) offers a helpful starting point to consider the above question. The word 'numeracy' is used in a broad sense covering all aspects of mathematics.

> *Numeracy at Key Stages 1 and 2 is a proficiency that involves a confidence and competence with numbers and measures. It requires an understanding of the number system, a repertoire of computational skills and an inclination and ability to solve number problems in a variety of contexts. Numeracy also demands practical understanding of the ways in which information is gathered by counting and measuring, and is presented in graphs, diagrams, charts and tables.* (p. 4)

A close look at the list of objectives for teaching numeracy, as presented in the *Framework for Teaching Mathematics* (DfEE 1999), will also show that the word numeracy is interpreted within this broader definition. The objectives are to:

- have a sense of the size of a number and where it fits into the number system;
- know by heart number facts such as number bonds, multiplication tables, doubles and halves;
- use what they know by heart to figure out answers mentally;
- calculate accurately and efficiently, both mentally and with pencil and paper, drawing on a range of calculation strategies;

- recognise when it is appropriate to use a calculator, and be able to do so effectively;
- make sense of number problems, including non-routine problems, and recognise the operations needed to solve them;
- explain their methods and reasoning using correct mathematical terms;
- judge whether their answers are reasonable and have strategies for checking them where necessary;
- suggest suitable units of measuring, and make sensible estimates of measurements;
- explain and make predictions from the numbers in graphs, diagrams, charts and tables.

For the purpose of writing this book we have adopted the above definition and objectives of teaching numeracy and this is, of course, reflected in the contents of the book.

In order to become effective teachers of mathematics we not only need to take note of the above list of objectives, but also consider elements of pedagogy. For this reason, in addition to elements directly relating to mathematical subject knowledge, we have also included a range of other issues such as problem solving, teaching of mental arithmetic, assessment of mathematical learning, progression, provision for low attainers and promising mathematicians and the use of ICT to enhance mathematical learning. We have attempted to *unlock* the teaching of numeracy by focusing on the following aspects:

- mathematics subject knowledge – what different mathematical ideas and terminology mean and what we need to understand to be able to offer high-quality teaching to children;
- specific needs of groups of children;
- practical ideas for teaching numeracy.

Following the implementation of the National Numeracy Strategy, there has been a large amount of published material available to teachers from the DfES, QCA as well as from commercial publishers. While the DfES and QCA publications offer structured support for classroom provision, most of the other materials offer good ideas for the classroom. Many schools have started using ready-made lesson plans. Most teachers feel that the in-service courses provided by the National Numeracy Strategy, through the Local Education Authorities (LEAs), have been very useful in delivering the numeracy strategy. However, during recent months, advisers from LEAs that work with Brunel University have been discussing the need for teachers to have opportunities to spend time thinking about some issues in more depth. Until three years ago, government-funded 10- and 20-day in-service courses offered teachers this opportunity. Recently, LEAs have commissioned us to deliver such courses. One of the aims of this book is to offer teachers opportunities to reflect on issues and promote debate. A balance of theory, reference to recent research and practical strategy is offered with the intention of supporting teachers to improve classroom practice.

The chapters in this book have been informed by the three interacting roles of the contributors – their many years of experience of providing mathematics in-service courses to hundreds of teachers, involvement in initial training of teachers and their own research into aspects of mathematics education. Some of the ideas introduced here are new and have not have been dealt with in other publications.

In Chapter 1, Bob Jeffery invites the reader to experience numeracy by trying out some tasks. He introduces aspects of teaching numeracy by explaining the underlying principles according to which we should teach numearcy. By doing the tasks, the reader will not only develop a robust understanding of concepts, but also appreciate the implications of teaching these concepts to children. The ideas developed in this chapter have been used as a basis of much of the mathematics teams' teaching of the in-service and initial training courses.

Mark Humble, in Chapter 2, provides a wealth of ideas to support the teaching of numeracy to older children. His ideas will not only provide significant practical help with classroom teaching, but also help to address issues of extension to Key Stage 3. The thrust of this chapter is on practical aspects of teaching numeracy and how teachers can maximise the effectiveness of their teaching.

In Chapter 3, Debbie Robinson considers some important issues relating to teaching mental mathematics. She facilitates analysis and reflection on two main questions: what are mental calculations and how can we teach mental calculations effectively? She places the teaching of mental mathematics within the main objectives for teaching mathematics and discusses elements of teaching styles and organisation that should enhance the effectiveness of classroom provision.

The positive role of ICT in the teaching of mathematics is undisputed. In Chapter 4, John Garvey explores the manner in which open-ended applications such as databases, spreadsheets and LOGO can enable children to understand and internalise mathematical concepts. It focuses on the strategies that teachers can use to allow children to tell the computer about their developing understanding of the mathematical world around them, drawing on established theories of learning and the development and representation of ideas.

In Chapter 5, Rachel Fairclough provides illuminating ideas on problem solving in mathematics and how these can be developed in children. Although problem solving is part of the numeracy strategy and is included in national initiatives such as World-Class tests, this topic has not received much attention recently. The author provides a framework for analysing different types of problems and invites the reader to consider what processes are involved in solving them.

Jean Murray considers issues relating to low attainment in mathematics in

Chapter 6. She uses case studies of a sample of underachieving children to analyse the nature of their difficulties and offers effective strategies to help them. Drawing on research and her own experience she tries to unlock the complexities of an area of mathematics which is of constant concern to all those involved in mathematics education. She raises and discusses a number of issues that should provide support to practising teachers in all phases of education.

Chapter 7 focuses on aspects of teaching mathematically promising students. Ron Casey introduces a model which has been successfully used by the Brunel Able Children's Education centre to enhance the quality of mathematics teaching for gifted mathematicians in several LEAs. He argues that provision for mathematically able pupils purely based on acceleration through the curriculum will stifle curiosity and creativity and may result in the superficial learning of ideas. The author offers an alternative model and gives reasons, with examples, for adopting this model in both teaching style and for the design of activities.

Valsa Koshy considers issues relating to assessment of mathematical learning in Chapter 8. She discusses the purposes of assessment within the planning, teaching and assessing cycle and focuses on the role of formative assessment in enhancing the quality of learning. Drawing on recent research and her own work, she provides a list of what constitutes good practice in formative assessment.

We hope this book will help to unlock aspects of numeracy support for all those who are involved in the teaching of mathematics, in their different roles. We have tried to make the style accessible and the ideas practical. Theory and research underpin our writing. We hope that our book will help the readers to think about issues in more depth and make more informed decisions in their teaching.

References

DfEE (1998) *The Implementation of the National Numeracy Strategy: The final report of the Numeracy Task Force*. London: Department for Education and Employment.

DfEE (1999) *Framework for Teaching Mathematics*. London: Department for Education and Employment.

CHAPTER 1

Aspects of numeracy

BOB JEFFERY

Introduction

Behind the apparently straightforward attributes of numeracy lie some rather puzzling features connected both with fundamental aspects of number and the complex historical background of present-day approaches. This chapter aims to set a context for the rest of the book by highlighting some of these aspects through a series of interactive exercises.

Numeracy comprises the knowledge, skills and understanding necessary to move around in the world of numbers with confidence and competence.

The term *confidence*, as used here implies a feeling of security, the ability to make connections between the various aspects of numeracy and the courage to develop personal methods and vary them according to the particular problem. *Making connections* is used rather than *understanding* since the latter term has a history of abuse in the teaching of mathematics as in 'Do you understand what I want you to do?' Many adults express quite the opposite of confidence about numeracy.

The chapter does not provide a comprehensive treatment, but the exercises are designed to help the reader build some connections between different strands and to develop a personal story about numeracy. In this respect, it is in line with the definition above. You do not become numerate without thinking for yourself and you cannot help others without some appreciation of potential difficulties.

The exercises require you to engage in mathematical thinking and to reflect on your own thoughts and experience. There is a commentary at the end.

To get the maximum benefit do the exercises before reading the commentary.

Exercise 1 – What is number?

Number is an abstract concept.

It is unfortunate that the term 'abstract' has become almost a term of abuse in the English language. However, mathematics is a subject which deals with abstract concepts and children work with abstract ideas in their earliest mathematical encounters.

Suppose you have just arrived from another planet and that you have no concept of number. You enter a world where everyone is talking about number using number names like one, two, three … What are the possible sources of confusion as you try to understand what is going on? You could start by thinking of someone pointing at a picture of three yellow ducks and saying 'three'. As far as you are concerned the word might mean *birds, ducks, yellow, dinner or three*! How can you learn what is meant by 'three'?

Does Erh mean 'two', 'red', or 'telephone box' in Chinese?

Exercise 2 – Mathematics in the mind

Try the following problem.

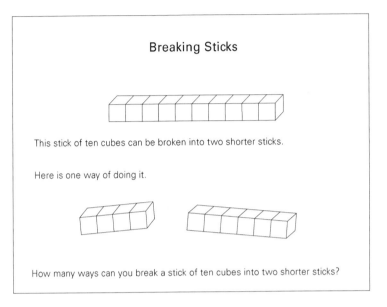

There are two different answers that are commonly given. What are they? Check with someone else if you can see only one answer. What is going on here and what has it got to do with the abstract? Did you stick with the physical problem or start playing with numbers?

Postscript
The picture shows the stick broken into six cubes and four cubes. The *difference* between six and four is two. Take a ten-stick and break it so that the *difference* is six. Try to do the same for differences four, eight and three. Make up a general rule about this activity. Note to what extent you rely on manipulating the cubes (perhaps in times of stress!) and what kind of thought experiments you make. Watching children do these activities will tell you quite a lot about their numeracy.

Exercise 3 – Counting

For this exercise to be effective you *must* count the squares in each box. Review your strategies and difficulties. You may find it useful to use terms such as:

One-to-one correspondence   Order   Pattern

Grouping   Counting in ....   Odd and even

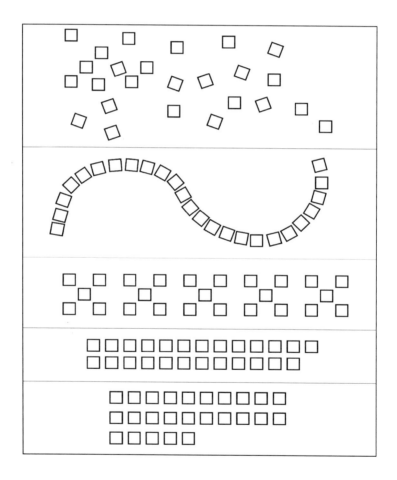

Exercise 4 – Fundamental ideas about number and number operations

Sit down with at least one friend and a box of mixed materials – any small objects that can be used for counting. It would be useful to have materials that possess a number of different attributes such as different colour or shape.

Try to use the materials to illustrate as many of these terms as possible.

Ordinal number, cardinal number
Counting
One-to-one correspondence
Counting on and counting back
Symbolism and numerals
Repeated addition
Repeated subtraction
Sharing
Addition, subtraction, multiplication, division
Odd and even
More than, fewer than
Grouping
Place value
The difference

Exercise 5 – Mental arithmetic – an investigation

For this activity you need at least one friend to help. The calculations should all be done mentally. There is no limit on time!

Do them one at a time and then compare notes about your methods after each one. Take your time to explore the differences fully, including the origins of your methodology, speed and accuracy, relationships with written calculations, mental images and personal feelings.

Add 18 and 14
From 125 subtract 88
26 multiplied by 9
105 divided by 13
From 152 subtract 63
48 multiplied by 12
132 divided by 4

Exercise 6 – With and without place value

Life is made easier by having a place value system of numeration, both for naming numbers and calculations. The Romans didn't crack this one!

A Roman nightmare

24 + 19 =   14 + 15 =   36 – 19 =

Convert these to Roman numerals, try the calculations and weep! The Hindu–Arabic system of numeration that we use offers some advantages. What are they? Discuss.

English	Chinese
One	E
Two	Erh
Three	San
Four	Ssu
Five	Wu
Six	Liu
Seven	Chi
Eight	Pa
Nine	Chiu
Ten	Shih
Fifteen	Shih Wu
Twenty	Erh Shih
Forty-five	Ssu Shih Wu
Fifty-one	Wu Shih E
Seventy-eight	Chi Shih Pa

What is thirty-two in Chinese? What is eighty-nine? How *did* you do it?

The number of numbers is infinite, so how is it that we can have a name for every number?

Investigate counting in some other languages. How much do you need to learn in order to count to one thousand?

Exercise 7 – Modelling number – place value 1

This commercially produced material is attributed to Z. P. Dienes and has its uses in helping to resolve problems about the nature and role of the place value system of numeration. Try these activities to learn something about the material and its potential.

Dienes Base 10

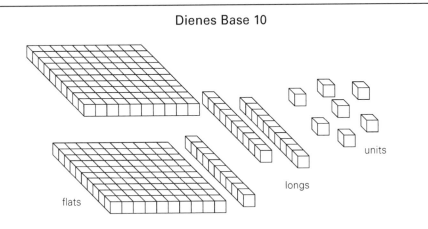

Big pile

Make a big pile of wood. See if you can simplify it so that you have the same amount of wood but fewer pieces.

Cube games (for two–four players)

Take turns to throw a die. The number you throw entitles you to add that number of units to your pile. The first person to make two longs is the winner.

Everyone starts with two longs and eight units. Take turns to throw a die. The number you throw tells you how many units to take away from your pile. The first person to get to zero is the winner.

The four rules

Explore how to model the four rules with Dienes. Try 'teaching' a friend. Note issues and questions for further discussion. Look to see how some mathematics schemes approach the use of Dienes.

Exercise 8 – Modelling number – place value 2

There are many materials that can be used to help resolve particular problems. Try these activities to learn something about the materials and their potential.

Counting Boards

Explore the use of counting boards with counters, coins, Dienes and numeral cards.

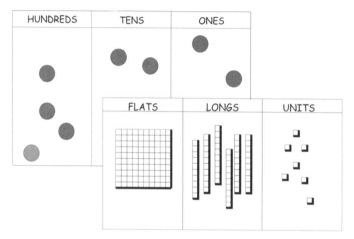

High and Lows – for two players
You need a counting board and 20 cards with the numerals 0–9 (two of each). Place the cards face down. Take turns to pick a card and place it in either the tens or the units position. The second card must be placed in the remaining place. Highest number wins (or lowest number, or nearest to 67 . . .)

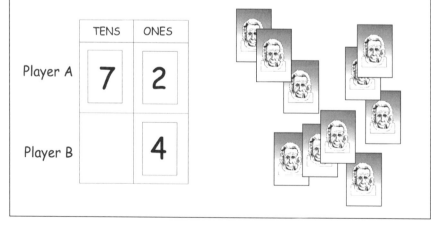

Exercise 9 – Modelling number – number lines and strips

Number lines and strips are just two ways of representing ideas about number and number operations. They can be useful as physical objects or as mental images. Explore their potential by engaging in the following activities.

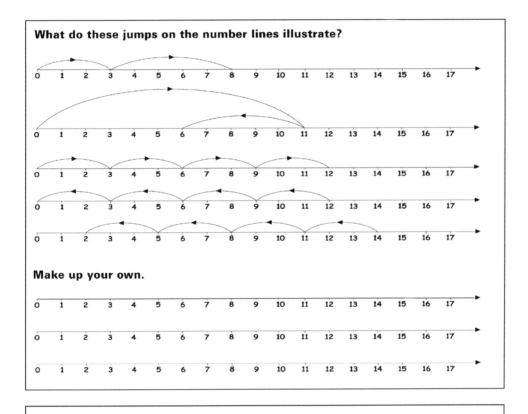

What do these jumps on the number lines illustrate?

Make up your own.

Twenty Questions

Think of a number and give your friends 20 questions (yes or no answers).

Explore any mental images they have. Discuss the implications for teaching.

Number strips

Imagine you are folding the number ...
   The crease is at 12 – what does 7 land on?
   4 lands on 22 – where does the crease come?

Exercise 10 – Tables

You should be familiar with the multiplication table square and its potential for stimulating thinking about numbers and number operations.

Investigate the patterns and symmetry – these can help in reconstructing forgotten facts.

Numbers may occur once, twice, three times, or more. What is the reason?

1	2	3	4	5	6	7	8	9	10	11	12
2	4	6	8	10	12	14	16	18	20	22	24
3	6	9	12	15	18	21	24	27	30	33	36
4	8	12	16	20	24	28	32	36	40	44	48
5	10	15	20	25	30	35	40	45	50	55	60
6	12	18	24	30	36	42	48	54	60	66	72
7	14	21	28	35	42	49	56	63	70	77	84
8	16	24	32	40	48	56	64	72	80	88	96
9	18	27	36	45	54	63	72	81	90	99	108
10	20	30	40	50	60	70	80	90	100	110	120
11	22	33	44	55	66	77	88	99	110	121	132
12	24	36	48	60	72	84	96	108	120	132	144

On the next few pages there are some challenges to help you see the potential of the multiplication square.

Exercise 11 – Building strategies for multiplication

The problem is how to learn to use the facts you know to generate the ones you don't know. Use this activity as the basis for discussion of how to set about it.

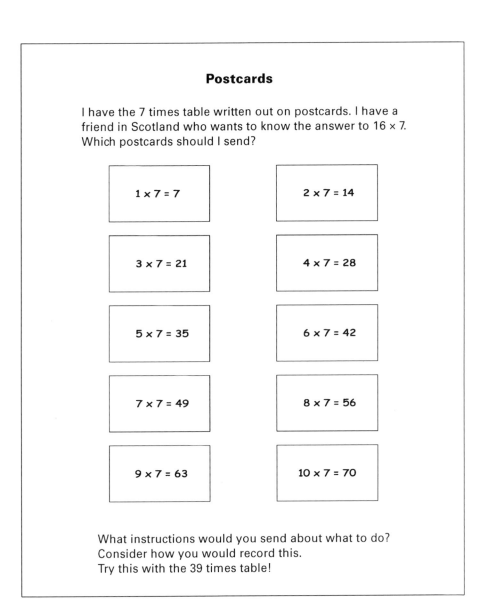

Postcards

I have the 7 times table written out on postcards. I have a friend in Scotland who wants to know the answer to 16 × 7. Which postcards should I send?

1 × 7 = 7	2 × 7 = 14
3 × 7 = 21	4 × 7 = 28
5 × 7 = 35	6 × 7 = 42
7 × 7 = 49	8 × 7 = 56
9 × 7 = 63	10 × 7 = 70

What instructions would you send about what to do?
Consider how you would record this.
Try this with the 39 times table!

Exercise 12 – Using a calculator to support mental arithmetic

There are many calculator activities that are aimed at developing mental arithmetic. Review the role of the calculator in this activity.

The Broken Calculator

Most of the buttons on your calculator are broken.

Only 2 3 8 + = are working.

How can you make 13 in the display?

Now try these. The Minimum number of button presses is best.

Use the buttons below to record your method.

11   31   61   240   464

Exercise 13 – Investigating number

Monitor your actions and thought processes – use this list to help you.

being playful
making categories
testing conjectures
explaining

asking questions
making conjectures (generalisations)
being persistent

Sometimes true, always true, never true

Check these out and explain
- the sum of consecutive odd numbers is a square number;
- the sum of 3 consecutive numbers is a multiple of three;
- the sum of 5 consecutive numbers is an odd number;
- the sum of 2 consecutive numbers is an odd number.

Consecutive Sums

These numbers are made from the sum of consecutive integers

$$7 = 3 + 4 \qquad 30 = 9 + 10 + 11 \qquad 15 = 1 + 2 + 3 + 4 + 5$$
$$14 = 2 + 3 + 4 + 5 \qquad 15 = 4 + 5 + 6$$

Investigate.

Happy Numbers

A number is HAPPY if the number chain made by summing the squares of the digits eventually leads to 1.

For example 23 is happy.

$$2^2 + 3^2 = 13 \qquad 1^2 + 3^2 = 10 \qquad 1^2 + 0^2 = 1$$

23 $\longrightarrow$ **13** $\longrightarrow$ **10** $\longrightarrow$ **1**

Of course, 13 and 10 are happy as well.

All numbers which are not happy are SAD. Find the happy and sad numbers which are less than 100.

Exercise 14 – Written algorithms

An arithmetical algorithm is a procedure for calculation.

There are several different algorithms that enable the same calculation to be performed. They all exploit the powerful features of our system of numeration (Hindu–Arabic), which is based on place value.

A 'standard' written algorithm is one that is commonly used and taught.

Effective 'personal' written algorithms (or variations on a standard algorithm) will also be encountered.

Teachers and schools have to make decisions about the relative importance they give to the development of standard and personal algorithms in their teaching.

This is not a trivial matter to determine.

What is your view about these attributes of written algorithms?

Essential, desirable, not essential – what do you think?

A written algorithm should

- be efficient (produce answers quickly);
- be effective (produce a high proportion of correct answers);
- be understood (an understanding of why it works, not just memorisation of the processes);
- be standardised so that all children learn the same algorithm;
- be based on the mental algorithms that children use;
- be invented by the learner.

Note: This is *not* a list of achievable characteristics, they are in conflict with each other. The challenge is to make the best compromise and maximise the desirable aspects.

Review your opinion after working through the next few pages.

Exercise 15 – What does rote learning feel like?

On this page you are invited to learn a new algorithm for subtraction.

A New Method of Subtraction

546 - 268 =

Subtract each digit in the smaller number from 9 and write the answers under the larger number.

546 - 268 =
731

Add

546 - 268 =
731
———
1277

Remove the 1 at the beginning and add it to the last digit

546 - 268 = 278
731
———
$\cancel{1}27\cancel{7}^{8}$

Now try some more!

Yes it does work! But why?

Exercise 16 – Written algorithms for subtraction – an exercise in morality?

This is a useful piece of historical information to help you interpret some of the subtraction algorithms you will find 'at large'. It is *not* a guide to how you should teach subtraction.

There are two popular written algorithms for subtraction in the adult community in the United Kingdom. They are called 'decomposition' and 'equal additions'. Decomposition is favoured in schools because it permits children to develop it themselves through the use of materials (e.g. Dienes Arithmetic Blocks). The understanding of why equal additions works is more difficult. Sadly, 'equal additions' is more likely to produce the correct answer – and produce it faster!

There are 'traditional mutters' that go with these methods and particularly with equal additions, with the terms 'borrowing' and 'paying back' prominent. Borrowing and paying back does not relate to *why* the algorithm works. The terms probably have their origin in Victorian strategies for remembering the algorithm by reference to well-known moral principles.

Somehow the term 'borrowing' has 'leaked' into the decomposition algorithm – with lack of morality because there is no 'paying back'! It would be sensible to use words and phrases such as 'break down the ten into ten ones' which relate more closely to what is happening.

Decomposition

64	$^5\!6^1\!4$	$^5\!6^1\!4$
- 28	- 28	- 28
		36
8 from four you can't	So you break down one of the tens into 10 units	8 from 14 is 6 2 from 5 is 3

Equal additions

64	$6^1\!4$	$6^1\!4$
- 28	- 28	- 28
	6	36
8 from four you can't	Borrow a one 8 from 14 is 6	Pay back (The two becomes 3 - not always indicated on paper) 3 from 6 is 3

Exercise 17 – The problem with division

The idea of 'sharing' develops from social activities and many children (and adults) persist in calling division 'sharing'. Unfortunately, the development of efficient mental algorithms is based more on the notions of *repeated subtraction*, *division as the inverse of multiplication* and *place value*.

Look carefully at the examples below and imagine that you are using the bricks to solve the problem (or use materials). Can you identify which one is 'repeated subtraction'?

---

24 ÷ 6 = 4

How many 6-brick towers can you make with 24 bricks?

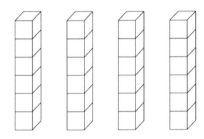

What do you count to find the answer?

Share 24 bricks equally between 6 children. How many do they get each?

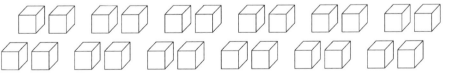

What do you count to find the answer?

Exercise 18 – Some language issues

Find language clues for the four rules – and look for misleading clues as well. Consider the kind of strategies that could be employed to clarify the issues – drawing pictures – visualising – materials. Discuss the implications for teaching.

Suppose you wanted to use a calculator to solve these boring simple problems. Which of the following would you enter?

$$12 + 3 = \qquad 12 - 3 = \qquad 12 \times 3 = \qquad 12 \div 3 =$$

There are 12 cows in a field. How many cows will be left when 3 have been taken away to market?

In a bus there are just 12 men and 3 women. How many people are there in the bus altogether?

If 12 sweets are shared equally between 3 children, how many does each receive?

There are 3 houses in a road and each house has 12 windows. How many windows altogether?

John lives at number 12 and Sushma lives at number 3. Where does Surjiben live?

A piece of rope 12 metres long is cut into 3 equal parts. How long is each part?

Wayne has saved up £3 to buy a game which costs £12. How much more money does he need?

Maggie has saved up £12 to buy a football. She still needs another £3. How much does the football cost?

Dan's pencil is 12 cm long and Maria's is only 3 cm long. How much longer is Dan's pencil than Maria's?

How many towers 3 bricks high can you build out of 12 bricks?

When 3 people are away from the office there are only 12 people left. How many people are there in the office when nobody is away?

How many 3 metre skipping ropes can you make from a piece of rope 12 metres long?

Jan has 3 cakes and each cake is divided into 12 pieces. How many pieces altogether?

A beetle is 3 cm long and a worm is 12 cm long. How many times as long as the beetle is the worm?

There are 12 different body colours and 3 different seat colours for a Ford car. How many different colour combinations are there?

Exercise 19 – Making sense of fractions

In these diagrams, the fractions are represented by area. There are many other ways of representing fractions (e.g. on number lines) and each one can help you develop your thinking about them.

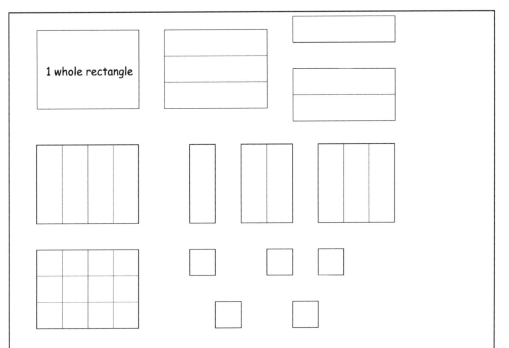

Find quarters, thirds, twelfths in these pictures.

$$\require{cancel} \cancel{\dfrac{1}{4} \; + \; \dfrac{2}{3} \; = \; \dfrac{3}{7}}$$

Why is this crazy? Use the pictures to support your arguments.

$$\dfrac{1}{4} \; + \; \dfrac{2}{3} \; = \; \dfrac{3}{12} \; + \; \dfrac{8}{12} \; = \; \dfrac{11}{12}$$

Why is this sensible? Use the pictures to support your arguments.

Notes

Exercise 1 – What is number?

Numbers used in this way tell us 'how many'. We call this aspect of number 'cardinality'. To learn about the cardinal number three you need to experience 'three-ness' in many different contexts. As well as cardinality, number is also used to describe order. Duck number three is the third duck.

Erh means two in Mandarin Chinese.

Exercise 2 – Mathematics in the mind

The two common answers to the first problem are 5 and 9. If you count breaking into 3 and 7 as being different from breaking into 7 and 3 you get 9. If you count them as the same you get 5. So, which is correct? Well, if you look at the words of the problem carefully and at the picture, you will see that there are nine places where the stick could be broken. If you got five, you should also be pleased because you have move into the abstract world and temporarily forgotten about the cubes – behaving just like a mathematician! Can you predict what would happen with 11 cubes or 20 cubes?

In the second activity you should reflect on the knowledge you have had to recall in order to find the answer. You are also asked to do the impossible – make a difference of 3. Can you make an argument about why this is impossible (think about odd and even numbers).

Exercise 3 – Counting

The answer is 35 in each case although this may not be suspected at a casual glance.

Counting can tell you about both cardinal (how many as in 'seven') and ordinal (order as in 'seventh'). You can count by making a one-to-one correspondence between a remembered list of names (one, two, three …) and actions such as pointing.

Some arrangements like the 'snake' make counting in this way easier. If you can move the objects it sometimes makes it easier – putting them into a bag as you count for example.

Most people learn to count in twos. If you play dominoes you learn to count in fives. Counting in tens is quite important in our system of writing numbers. These experiences help in some of the other counts on this page.

Exercise 4 – Fundamental ideas about number and number operations

Explorations like this can help to provide a secure foundation for the development of abstract thinking.

Exercise 5 – Mental arithmetic – an investigation

Unless you have been rather unlucky, this should have revealed a variety of methods. Some people are more comfortable with mental methods which mirror those that they use with pencil and paper. On the other hand, others select strategies which are suited to the particular calculation. For example, some people add in order to subtract!

Lurking in the background is our place value system of numeration based on ten.

Exercise 6 – With and without place value

Poor old Romans! You should be able to count in Chinese because the system, based on grouping in tens is the same as ours. It is called 'place value' because in any numeral, each digit's value is determined by its place or position. For example in 333 the first 3 mean '3 hundreds', the second one means '3 tens' and the final one '3 units'. The systematic way of recording numbers in units, tens, hundreds and so on makes it easy for us to contemplate continuing the process for larger and larger numbers.

Exercises 7 and 8 – Modelling number – place value

The relative size of the Dienes pieces makes it clear that you could be in trouble if you mistake hundreds for units! These activities are designed to explore place value in action. Some of the strategies you will use provide the basis for written algorithms.

Exercise 9 – Modelling number – number lines and strips

Addition, subtraction, multiplication, division (repeated subtraction) and division with a remainder are all represented here.

Many people report 'seeing' number lines when they are working on numerical problems.

Review your strategies for solving the problems with number strips. Can you refine them?

Exercise 10 – Tables

This page is all about multiplication facts. Memorisation of all the results is useful, but time spent exploring the derivation of the results and the patterns they make can help you to quickly construct the ones you have forgotten.

Also, explorations like this provide activity typical of mathematical problem solving.

Exercise 12 – Using a calculator to support mental arithmetic

Common criticism of the use of calculators in education is focused on the negative aspects of dependence. However the calculator can be used to support the development of mental arithmetic strategies as these activities show.

The calculator provides the stimulus for some mental arithmetic and a means of checking answers. Note how useful it is to have committed some facts to memory and to some ideas of patterns to expect. In the broken calculator activity however, it is worth checking your answers with someone else. Don't forget you can use the buttons to make numbers with more than one digit such as 238, 833 and 32.

Exercise 13 – Investigating number

Arithmetic offers far more than utilitarian calculations. There are some interesting phenomena to explore. There are no 'answers' to these investigations! You have to make up your own questions and explore them. 'Consecutive sums' gives opportunities for employing a typical range of strategies. Check your own against the following list (not necessarily in order):

Being playful, generating results, recording results, being systematic, tabulating results, specialising (looking at particular kinds of numbers), making conjectures (about general rules), testing conjectures (to see if they apply universally), explaining.

For 'happy numbers' you need to persist with the numbers until you are certain that they are identified correctly. Make a picture to show the sad numbers.

Exercise 15 – What does rote learning feel like?

This illustrates some of the tensions on page 14. If you got the feeling that you were not in control of the situation you will understand how children might feel if algorithms are produced from nowhere. On the other hand, this, like many algorithms is efficient and always works. If you want a clue as to why it works, crossing out the 1 at the beginning is equivalent to subtracting 1000 and adding one at the end is equivalent to adding one unit – a net result of subtracting 999. If you can work out why the first result is always 999 too big (in three-digit calculations) you have done it. How does it work in two digits?

Exercise 16 – Written algorithms for subtraction

Explore the written algorithms used by your friends for multiplication, subtraction and division. Find out about the origins of these.

Exercise 17 – The problem with division

Use any insight you get from this to examine you own strategies for division.

Exercise 18 – Some language issues

You will note here that some of the obvious clue words, such as 'divided' do not necessarily point to the correct operation. Collect your own examples.

Exercise 19 – Making sense of fractions

This activity is designed to help you come to terms with some of the common problems and misconceptions with fractions.

CHAPTER 2

Investigating numeracy in Key Stage 2

MARK HUMBLE

Introduction

The application of mathematical knowledge, or what in the 1989 and 1995 versions of the National Curriculum for primary mathematics in England and Wales (DES 1989; DfE 1995) was termed 'using and applying mathematics', has long been recognised as an important aspect of the development of mathematical thinking. Superficially, this aspect continues to be of importance in the National Numeracy Strategy (DfEE 1999b) through the 'solving problems' strand. As Hughes *et al.* (2000) state, however,

> *a closer examination of the key objectives of the Numeracy Framework ... raises concern that in practice there will be an over-riding emphasis on number knowledge and calculation skills, with relatively little attention being given to application.*
>
> (2000:35)

In the National Curriculum (DfEE 1999a) there is no separate section of the programmes of study for Ma 1 (using and applying mathematics, the first attainment target); rather the teaching requirements relating to this attainment target are permeated into the programmes of study for number, shape, space and measures, and data handling. The omission of such pedagogical guidance gives unfortunate messages about the lack of importance of using and applying mathematics in children's learning. The effects of this omission in practice will be compounded by the fact that this is a particularly challenging area of the mathematics curriculum that many teachers have found difficult to teach (see Hughes *et al.* 2000).

This chapter reasserts the importance of giving children opportunities to apply and use their mathematical knowledge and understanding through an appropriate range of problem-solving and investigative activities. It argues that knowledge and understanding of numeracy *and* the skills of mathematical thinking can be simultaneously developed and enriched through the use of appropriate learning contexts. In particular, it offers an example of how one teaching resource can be used as a context for numeracy work in Key Stage 2 that

- develops and enriches awareness of the inter-related world of number;
- includes opportunities for developing thinking through the processes involved in making and monitoring mathematical decisions and communicating mathematically;
- enables children to be creative in their mathematical work;
- provides links to early algebra work through the processes of pattern spotting and reasoning, proof and logic.

The chapter is structured as follows: a brief analysis of mathematical application work explains and justifies this approach to numeracy. This is followed by an outline of the teaching resource and of the possible different ways of using it. The mathematical potential of some of the activities is then discussed and illustrated.

The application and use of mathematical knowledge

Askew (1998:159) identifies three areas within the using and applying aspect of mathematics: making and monitoring decisions, mathematical communication and reasoning, logic and proof. The first of these areas means that children need opportunities to make decisions about the appropriate mathematics to use, and to check that these decisions are sensible. The second involves offering children the opportunity to talk, read and write about the mathematics they have used. Reasoning, logic and proof involves 'being able to make simple generalisations, hypotheses and argue through results' (p. 159).

At the heart of this aspect of mathematics is the need to provide children with well-structured learning contexts in which their existing mathematical knowledge and thinking can be applied, developed and enriched. Contexts need to be varied, motivating, challenging and capable of providing a sense of mathematical 'discovery'.

The teaching resource used as the starting context for all of the investigations detailed below is a set of carpet tiles, numbered from 1 to 100 and set out in a 100 grid (see Figure 2.1). The tiles provide opportunities for investigating 'within mathematics itself' (Askew 1998:158). As the ideas below show, they offer a large number of ways in which children can be challenged to make decisions, to search for patterns and generalisations, to make hypotheses, to discuss and communicate their ideas, and to develop simple ideas of proof. There are also opportunities for children to explore and develop their ideas about the structure of the numbers and the number operations involved.

In a study of effective teachers of numeracy, Askew *et al.* (1997) found that one of the characteristics of such teachers was the ways in which they established connections within the mathematics curriculum, enabling their pupils to understand the rich and inter-connected world of numeracy. The carpet tiles investigations therefore offer ways of simultaneously developing numeracy know-ledge and the processes that are part of mathematical thinking.

91	92	93	94	95	96	97	98	99	100
81	82	83	84	85	86	87	88	89	90
71	72	73	74	75	76	77	78	79	80
61	62	63	64	65	66	67	68	69	70
51	52	53	54	55	56	57	58	59	60
41	42	43	44	45	46	47	48	49	50
31	32	33	34	35	36	37	38	39	40
21	22	23	24	25	26	27	28	29	30
11	12	13	14	15	16	17	18	19	20
1	2	3	4	5	6	7	8	9	10

Figure 2.1

All of the investigations start with practical work on the carpet tiles. These starting points offer children the kinaesthetic and visual experiences which the pedagogical guidance of the NNS (1999b) identifies as important for all learners. Additionally, they offer a different and large-scale experience of mathematics. As Potworowski (1991:18) identifies in school mathematics work, the motto often seems to be think small, not 'think big', and for most children,

> the field of action shrinks to a space of about 25cm by 25cm, heads go down, fingers grip pens, shoulders hunch up and melancholia sets in.

Most mathematics work is not only small scale, but even when purporting to be a group endeavour, it is actually solitary and focused on individual achievement. In contrast, practical work with the carpet tiles offers the starting point of a large-scale, communal experience of investigating mathematics. This starting point can then be taken into smaller-scale, pair or individual work, as and when appropriate, using a printed 100 grid. The practical work becomes the starting point, and provides an interesting and relevant scaffold for the mathematical thinking.

In the next section each teaching idea is outlined, together with some key teacher questions identified in bold. The mathematical potential within each idea is then identified and discussed.

Ways of using the carpet tiles

Multiply Me

Practical Work

Split the class into two equal groups. One group will observe. Each member of the other group stands on a tile, starting from 1 and making sure that all the successive tiles are used. These children are then asked to move to the tile that is their number ×2. Before any movement occurs, predictions can be made both about individual numbers and about the general pattern that will occur on the grid.

What will your new number be?
What number will the person next to you move to?
What pattern might we make on the grid?

Once movement is allowed, it is helpful if children standing on the highest numbers move first to prevent chaos! The pattern of bodies on the grid now needs to be considered.

Why has this pattern happened?
What operation will enable you to return to your original position?

Using this operation the children return to their original tiles and repeat the exercise, but this time with multiplication by 3.

What will your new number be?
What number will the person next to you move to?
What pattern might we make on the grid?
Why is this pattern different?
What will happen if you multiply your original number by 4? 5?

A smaller-scale option is for ten members of the class to stand on the tiles numbered 1 to 10, while the rest of the class observe. This option can be useful for exploring other multiples – 9 is particularly good to try.

Mathematical Potential

The children are clearly working on their multiplication tables. However, at the same time, through this physical approach, a feeling for the divergence of multiplication is experienced. To start with, the children are standing shoulder to shoulder and as each multiplication is applied the gaps between them increases. As they spread out a pattern representing their position becomes obvious. For example, multiplication by two produces vertical columns whereas multiplication by three has a diagonal or sloping feel to the pattern. The children should be encouraged to describe and explain these patterns.

For the children to return to their original tile after multiplication requires them to divide, division being the inverse operation for multiplication. This act reinforces the purpose of inverse operations and can be built on in the next activity.

Multiply Me. Then Multiply Me Again

Practical Work

If you have previously been working with only a small group then swap groups now. Children assemble as before starting at 1. These children are asked to multiply their number by 3 and move to the tile equivalent to the answer and then multiply that tile by 2.

What will your final number be?
What will your neighbour's final numbers be?
What pattern might we make?

The children should now be allowed to move to the final tile and, with the observers, consider the pattern created.

Can you describe the pattern generated?
Can you explain this pattern drawing on the outcomes of the previous activity?
What *single* operation will enable you to return to your original tile?

Using this operation the children return to their original tiles and repeat the exercise, but this time with multiplication by 4 and 2. Clearly with this calculation some children will be forced to move off the 100 square. This does not matter but a smaller group of, say ten, could be used to develop this activity, if appropriate.

What will your new final number be?
What number will the person next to you move to?
What pattern might we make on the grid? Why is this pattern different?
What will happen if you multiply your original number by 4 then 2?

Mathematical Potential

The main fact to be learnt from this activity is that when you multiply by one number then another it is like multiplying by the product of those numbers. This is clarified when the children are asked to look for the single operation that is the inverse of multiplying by 3 then 2. The children should realise that the inverse is to divide by 6 because multiplying by 3 then 2 is like multiplying by 6. It is also valuable to note that the pattern derived from multiplying by 3 then 2 is a combination of the patterns that were generated in the previous activity when multiplying separately by 3 and 2, i.e. a combination of parallel columns with a diagonal feel – the six times table.

Multiply Me then Add to Me

Practical Work

Swap groups again with the new group forming up as before on the 100 square. This time the children are asked to multiply the number they are standing on by 2 and add 3 to that total. This is in preparation to moving to the tile that represents their answer.

What will your new number be?
What number will your neighbours move to?
What pattern might we make on the grid?

The children should now be allowed to move to their calculated tile and look back at the pattern to see if their predictions were correct.

Describe the new pattern.
What specific facts do you note about the new pattern?

To arrive at the tile you are now on you multiplied by 2 and added 3 – what operations will return you to where you started?

After discussing their thoughts, the children should be allowed to apply their inverse operations to test whether they do in fact return to their original tile.

Mathematical Potential

The combination of multiplication and addition will create patterns in terms of odd and even numbers. For example, multiplying by 2 and adding 3 will create the vertical column pattern experienced when multiplying by 2, but adding 3 will now situate the columns on odd numbers rather than even. The children need to be encouraged to explain why this is so, drawing on their knowledge of odd and even numbers.

The search for an inverse to multiplying by 2 and adding 3 is not simply a matter of dividing by 2 and subtracting 3 (a common misconception). This activity emphasises the fact that while the operations themselves have to be inversed so does the order of the operations in order to return to the original tile. Other combinations of the four operations will through experimentation support this fact.

Digital Roots

Practical Work

For this you can use the whole class by asking them to stand anywhere on the 100 square. Explain that digital roots for any number are found by adding its digits together until a single digit (1–9) is reached.

What do you think will happen if we all move to the digital root of our numbers?

Why do you feel this to be the case?

The children should now be encouraged to do their calculations and move accordingly. They should be encouraged to form lines behind these digits in the style of a human block graph.

What do you notice about the human block graph you are creating?

If we had 100 children standing on the 100 square what sort of shape do you think the block graph would be?

Explain your theory.

Mathematical Potential

Digital roots may be a new idea and needs to be carefully explained. It will however produce some useful practice of addition sums, but more importantly it will encourage the children to think about why certain outcomes arise. The block graph will reinforce work done in handling data, but it is predicting and explaining its shape that will generate the most numeracy debates.

By considering the numbers in the 100 grid and their location, digital root sums create diagonals which, when analysed, make it clear that the block graph should be rectangular with the number 1 having just one more 'block' to it. A triangular distribution of blocks is often put forward as the shape for the graph, but this can clearly be seen to be false.

Blindfolded

Practical Work

Six volunteers are selected to stand in the middle of the 100 square in a 2 by 3 rectangle. These children are all blindfolded and encouraged to link arms in their rows. Back and front rows also need to be linked. The best way to do this is to ask the children in the back row to place their free hands on the shoulders of the children in front of them. This 2 by 3 unit are then given a number of calculations to do for which they must move as one to their final position. Before any movement takes place a leader is chosen to orchestrate the moves. An example of a series of instructions are shown below:

1. Add 1 to your totals and move to that position.
2. Subtract 4 from this current total and move to the new position.
3. Add 10 to the current position and move to the new position.
4. Subtract 9 from the current position and move to the new position.

What do you predict will happen?
Why is it harder to do subtraction?

Mathematical Potential

To do this efficiently, the children must have a clear understanding of the structure of the 100 square, and be given time to discuss and argue with other members of the team of 6 to ensure that the movement is both correct and carried out unanimously. For example, to add any number less than 6 you move to the right and to subtract any number less than six you move to the left. However, to add or subtract 10 you simply take one step forward or one step backwards. The tricky move to predict then is that of subtracting 9. Clearly you must step back one tile but do you then move to the left or the right?

Square Dancing – Looking at Diagonals

Practical Work

Ask the children to form up in square groups of four (2 by 2) on the 100 square. One child on each diagonal is issued a calculator. The groups are then encouraged to describe what they see beneath their feet paying special attention to the diagonals.

What do you notice about the arrangement of numbers that you are standing on?

What do you notice when you add the diagonals? Is it the same for all the groups?

Why is this the case?

What do you notice when you multiply the diagonals? Is it the same for all the groups?

Why is this the case?

The children's explanations need careful consideration and should be discussed thoroughly before moving on to the next task. Now ask the children to maintain their square arrangement but to expand it to form a 3 by 3 square.

What do you notice about the arrangement of numbers that you are standing on?

What do you notice when you add the diagonals? Is it the same for all the groups?

Why is this the case?

What do you notice when you multiply the diagonals? Is it the same for all the groups?

Why is this the case?

After this discussion the children need to continue this line of enquiry using paper, pencil and calculator methods back at their tables.

Mathematical Potential

It is the structure of the 100 square that explains the outcomes that the children should encounter. Certainly it should be easy for the children to justify that when adding the diagonals the totals will always be the same. Also the expansion of the 'square' to 3 by 3 and beyond will produce the same result, regardless as to whether you include the additional numbers that occur on the diagonals or not. It is worth mentioning at this point that using digital roots will produce similar results and dovetails nicely with this activity.

It is the multiplication of the diagonals that produces more interesting points. When multiplying the diagonals of the 2 by 2 square there is a difference of ten in the totals obtained (digital roots will produce a difference of 1). Moving to the 3 by 3 square the difference becomes 40 (digital roots difference is 4). The following table shows the developing pattern more clearly and offers an algebraic explanation:

Size of square	Difference in numerical totals	Explanation	Difference in digital root totals
2 by 2	10	1×10	1
3 by 3	40	4×10	4
4 by 4	90	9×10	9
5 by 5	160	16×10	16
n by n		$(n-1)(n-1) \times 10$	$(n-1)(n-1)$

An obvious question that arises from this is why does the numerical difference mimic the square number sequence, but with a multiplier of 10 being applied? To find an answer to this, use the fact that the carpet tiles can be moved to produce new number squares – for example, one based on seven rather than ten. This configuration is found in daily life as the calendar and copies of months issued to children will enable them to investigate the phenomenon. Below is a table showing the results:

Size of square	Difference in numerical totals	Explanation
2 by 2	7	1×7
3 by 3	28	4×7
4 by 4	63	9×7
5 by 5	112	16×7
n by n		$(n-1)(n-1) \times 7$

The children are now in a position to investigate this problem further to establish the theory or proof and at the same time look at the limitations of the task (note for example that digital root differences are not considered this time).

Conclusion

This chapter has shown that knowledge and understanding of numeracy *and* the skills of mathematical thinking can be simultaneously developed and enriched through the use of appropriate learning contexts. It has shown how the teaching resource of numbered carpet tiles can be used as the starting point for the investigation of various aspects of numeracy in Key Stage 2. Such investigative work has the potential to develop and enrich children's awareness of the inter-related world of number. It also includes opportunities for developing thinking through the processes involved in making and monitoring mathematical decisions, and communicating mathematically. Such mathematical thinking links to early algebra work through the important processes of pattern spotting and reasoning, proof and logic. Finally, investigating within mathematics in this way enables children to be creatively challenged in their numeracy work.

Acknowledgements

The ideas detailed here were originally developed by Jan Potworowski from a presentation at an Association of Mathematics Teachers conference. They have been developed by Jan and by successive generations of staff, students and teachers on INSET courses at West London Institute of Higher Education and Brunel University.

References

Askew, M. (1998) *Teaching Primary Mathematics*. London: Hodder and Stoughton.

Askew, M., Brown, M., Rhodes, V., Wiliam, D. and Johnson, D. (1997) *Effective Teachers of Numeracy: Report of a study carried out for the Teacher Training Agency*. London: King's College, University of London.

Department of Education and Science (DES) (1989) *Mathematics in the National Curriculum*. London: HMSO.

Department for Education (DfE) (1995) *Mathematics in the National Curriculum*. London: HMSO.

Department for Education and Employment (DfEE) (1999a) *Curriculum 2000*. London: DfEE.

Department for Education and Employment (DfEE) (1999b) *The National Numeracy Strategy: Framework for Teaching Mathematics from Reception to Year 6*. London: DfEE.

Hughes, M., Desforges, C., Mitchell, C. with Carre, C. (2000) *Numeracy and Beyond: Applying Mathematics in the Primary School*. Milton Keynes: Open University Press.

Potworowski, J. (1991) 'Leaps and Bounds'. *Junior Education*, November.

CHAPTER 3

Teaching mental calculations

DEBBIE ROBINSON

How did you work that out?

As both a mother and a teacher of mathematics I am always keen to follow my own children's progress in mathematics. My three-year-old daughter Helen is beginning her development of mathematical understanding and happily chants the numbers one to ten and randomly assigns numbers to collections of objects. I have been particularly interested to observe the impact of the National Numeracy Strategy through my eight-year-old son Robert as he develops mathematical understanding and attitudes. This has been of great help to me in my own work as a teacher trainer in schools and university.

At home during a lengthy 'chat' with Robert about his mathematics, I asked him to tell me the answer to 23×4. He nodded and looked away as though deliberately avoiding eye contact and possibly further dialogue or interruption from me as he concentrated. Little was revealed from his fixed gaze beyond my right shoulder. Then he looked back to me and correctly replied '92'. The inevitable question from the mathematics teacher arrived: 'How did you work that out?' After a quick groan he explained that he had doubled and doubled again, and then pleaded, 'Can I go now? *Please*!' I knew when 'my time was up' and I allowed him to escape!

This conversation with my son had left me with many questions. I had intended to explore Robert's strategies for carrying out mental calculations. However, I was unsure about exactly what mathematical activity had been going on in his head. Telling me how he worked it out had not explained what thought processes he had been engaged in. I had accepted his explanation that he had doubled and doubled again. How exactly had he doubled? I began to scrutinise my own understanding of the exact 'nature' of mental calculations. Further, to speculate on how children learn to carry out mental calculations and how this learning fits into the 'big picture' of mathematics in schools.

For these reasons, therefore, this chapter sets out to consider two particular questions:

> **What is mental calculation?**
> **How can we teach mental calculation?**

What is mental calculation?

Despite its obvious current importance in the school curriculum it is difficult to find a precise definition for mental calculation. Considering mental calculation in relation to the following other mathematical terms might help to reveal its meaning:

- *written calculations;*
- *mental arithmetic;*
- *school mathematics;*
- *mental calculations.*

Written calculations

Written calculations appear to require the recording of working and the adherence to a standard accepted method of computation.
For example:

> *Given the question 23 + 38, using the standard written algorithm from addition, the numbers can be rewritten vertically.*
>
> $$\begin{array}{r} 23 \\ + 38 \\ \hline 61 \\ \hline \end{array}$$

Understanding 23 as 2 tens and 3 units and 38 as 3 tens and 8 units is necessary to enable the numbers to be appropriately arranged in columns and added correctly. This 'layout' of the numbers and the addition of two and three single digits, moving from left to right in order to allow the necessary carrying from the units to the tens column, gives the answer 61.

In contrast, when the calculation is made mentally, there is no necessity either to resort to the use of pen and paper or to use a particular method. In this instance 23 is considered as 20 and 3 and 38 as 30 and 8. This subtly different interpretation of the place value of the numbers, involved in the written as opposed to the mental calculation methods, is highlighted by Thompson (1999). Here the more significant numbers 20 and 30 can be added to give 50 first, followed by the totaling of the units 3 and 8 equaling 11. This allows the final answer to be reached by adding 50, 10 and 1. This contrasts with the written approach dictating the addition of columns of numbers from left to right allowing the collection of additional tens from the units column and so on. Further, without the requirement to classify the value of numbers into columns headed by powers of ten, each number may be considered in a wealth of different ways. So, 23 could be thought of as 20 and 3, as well as any number of alternate combinations. These might include, for example, 10 and 13, 22 and 1 or even 20 and 2 and 1. This flexibility in the understanding of composition of numbers encourages and allows much greater freedom in the approach to finding the answer to any given question. Without the necessity to consider numbers in terms of the tens and units, a wealth of number relationships can be utilised. In this particular example pairs of numbers that add to give ten might encourage the re-organisation of the sum as 38 + 20 + 2 + 1.

> *This enables counting on in tens (38 + 20 = 58),*
> *then up to a multiple of ten (58 + 2 = 60),*
> *before the addition of the extra one (60 + 1 = 61).*

Are written calculations unlike mental calculations essentially because of the interpretation of the place value of the numbers involved? The successful application of a standard written algorithm is dependent on a specific interpretation of the place value. In contrast the freedom to choose how to partition the numbers involved (i.e. other than as tens and units) enables great flexibility in the possible methods of solution. Does this mean that using mental calculations is essentially about the freedom to use 'informal' rather than a necessity to use 'formal' ways of working?

As part of my work with teachers, I have asked them to answer numerical questions in their heads, without writing anything down. They then compare and contrast their methods in order to analyse the understanding and strategies they have demonstrated. On many occasions, as teachers explained how they calculated the answer, some confessed that they had carried out the calculation in their head, but as a written sum. They kept track of their working with a mental picture of the standard algorithm, sometimes even including parallel lines for the answer, with small 'carried' figures below. These teachers had defaulted to a method and understanding of place value dictated by written calculations. They had simply held their workings in their head, rather than recording them with pen and paper. So, using a written method may not necessarily involve writing workings down. Conversely, writing workings down may preclude being engaged in mental calculation. In fact recording can be of great value in both the teaching and learning of mental calculations.

For example:

The use of empty number lines, would be a most effective way of demonstrating possible strategies for calculating the answer to 23 + 38

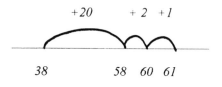

Figure 3.1

Start by marking 38 (the more significant figure) on the empty number line, an initial jump of + 20 is made to 58. Now, the addition of the three more needs to be made. By jumping + 2 up to 60 (achieved using bridging through a multiple of ten), followed by the final + 1, the answer is 61. Encouraging children to use an empty number line helps them structure their approach and the evidence provided by their recording illustrates their thinking.

While written calculations may not necessarily involve writing workings down, carrying out mental calculations may not preclude the use of pen and paper to keep track of workings. The essential difference is in the opportunity to structure and think about numbers and methods with flexibility and originality.

Mental arithmetic

Mental arithmetic could be considered as the ability to use 'mental dexterity' in the solution of numerical questions. In order to illustrate this, consider the question 16×15. A reasonable method of solution might be to restructure the problem as:

> $16 \times (10 + 5);$
> *leading to* $(16 \times 10) + \frac{1}{2} (16 \times 10);$
> *and then to add* $160 + 80 = 240.$

A sound understanding of place value and the laws of arithmetic are essential to understand this method. The distributive law allows 16×15 to equal $16 \times (10 + 5)$. Next the identification and use of the relationship between 6×10 and 16×5 allows greater ease in the calculation of $16 \times 10 = 160$ and then

16×5 as half of 160 (since 5 is half of 10). The correct recall of relevant memorised number facts together with the appropriate and competent completion of number operations allows the solution to be performed with both speed and accuracy.

How does mental calculation differ for mental arithmetic? It may be possible to make the distinction based on the particular context in which the child is working. If the answer to 16×15 had been found using the method described above, the child's recent previous learning experiences may be relevant. If the question follows repeated practice of this specific strategy, it is more likely that the approach has been implied rather than selected. Further, the teacher expectations critically influence the nature of the child's response. So if the teacher appears to value the speed and accuracy of the answer, the child may elect to use a strategy they are more familiar and confident with. Conversely, if the teacher explains that they are interested in *how* they worked it out and the reasons for their choice, the child may be encouraged to think more independently and imaginatively. *For example:*

> *In the solution of 16×15:*
>
> > *the proximity to a near known square $15 \times 15 = 225$,*
> > *followed by the addition of another 15,*
> > *gives $225 + 15 = 240$.*

Alternately, the factorisation of both or one of the numbers could allow the re-ordering of products to be more calculated with greater ease. *For example:*

> *16×15 could become:*
>
> > *$(2 \times 8) \times (3 \times 5)$,*
> > *allowing $(2 \times 5) \times (3 \times 8)$,*
> > *making $10 \times 24 = 240$.*

The preference of one approach over another will be determined by many factors and often reveals the child's experience and understanding of the number system, memorised facts, number relationships and strategies. The most 'appropriate' deployment of a particular approach is made in relation to each specific problem. There is still the desire to be efficient in terms of speed and accuracy, but an additional aspiration for mathematical 'elegance' is added: a desire to consider and capitalise on a broader perspective of mathematical relationships and systems. Could mental calculation be about valuing the quality of the process as well as the correctness of the product?

School mathematics

In a recent conversation a colleague persuaded me that mathematics by necessity must be mental. He argued that since mathematics is purely abstract and we use language and notations to discuss and record the process – in its broadest sense *all* mathematics is about activities that take place in the head.

Ernest (2000) identifies several 'components' that can be learnt in school mathematics. These are facts, skills, concepts and conceptual structures, strategies, attitudes to, and appreciation of, mathematics. Ernest also makes connections between the different components of mathematics and how they might expect to be learnt and therefore possibly taught in school with reference to the Cockcroft Report (1982, Para 243). The following table attempts to summarise and structure these ideas in relation to mental calculation.

Table 3.1   School mathematics: implications for learning and teaching

Component and Definition	Implied Learning *and Teaching Style*
Facts are 'atoms' of knowledge. *For example: number bonds and multiplication facts.*	Can be memorised with *teacher exposition, followed by practice and application through problem solving.*
Skills are well defined multi-step Procedures. *For example: Adding three and two digit numbers.*	Are often mastered by *exposition followed by practice and application through problem solving.*
Concepts are sets or properties that reveal ideas about meaning behind names. **Conceptual Structures** are sets of concepts with linking relationships. *For example: Place value of a single unit (3) and then its value within the whole number system (3, 30, 300, 0.3, –3 etc...)*	Are evolved and continue to develop through a range of experiences including *discussion, exposition, practical work, problem solving and investigational work.*
Strategies are procedures that guide the choice of skills or knowledge to use when problem solving. *For example: Using compensation to add (i.e. adding 19 by 20 then subtracting 1).*	They are usually learnt by example then refined and extended through application in *exposition, discussion, practical work, problem solving and investigational work.*
Attitudes to mathematics are the learner's feelings and responses. *For example: Striving for 'elegance' in choice and application of strategies in relation to specific questions.*	Formed and effected indirectly by the breadth and quality of mathematical experiences provided in *exposition, discussion, practical work, problem solving and investigational work.*
Appreciation of mathematics involves awareness of its value and role in life and what mathematics is as a whole. *For example: Ideas about infinity that are based on a genuine inquisitiveness.*	Developed informally through the presentation of work through *exposition, discussion, practical work, problem solving and investigational work.*

So this table shows that mental calculation involves learning and teaching in every component of school mathematics.

Mental calculations

In primary schools today, numeracy and in particular mental calculation are central parts of the mathematics curriculum. Common elements in the development of mental arithmetic, written and mental calculations could include:

- recall of memorised facts;
- mental dexterity with number skills and strategies;
- development of conceptual structures about number;
- helpful methods of recording workings.

In both mental arithmetic and mental calculation, speed and accuracy in finding solutions is important. However, mental calculation also involves the learning and teaching of positive attitudes to, and appreciation of, mathematics. A particular perception of mathematics is needed to be an effective mental calculator. The feelings and understandings of the subject cannot be taught in the same way as can facts, skills, strategies and concepts. Rather they are developed by good example in quality and breadth of teaching and learning experiences.

How can we teach mental calculation?

My work in schools has provided me with opportunities to observe children who are very able mental calculators. Exactly how they acquire their abilities is uncertain. Some children seem to learn mental effective methods for mental calculations without direct teaching or even guidance. However, the majority of children will need support. There are many different opinions on what form this help might take. Before offering my own ideas on the teaching of mental calculations it may be helpful to consider:

- the characteristics of an effective mental calculator;
- how children learn.

The characteristics of an effective mental calculator

Learning and teaching in components of school mathematics was considered earlier in this chapter. In my experience children who are effective mental calculators display particular characteristics in relation to each of the components: skills and facts, conceptual structures and strategies and attitudes to and appreciation of mathematics.

Table 3.2   Characteristics of an effective mental calculator

In the knowledge of facts and skills, they demonstrate:
- ability to recall useful number facts;
- accuracy in computation.

In understanding apply conceptual structures and strategies, they show:
- strong concept of place value;
- useful vocabulary to discuss their ideas;
- 'feel' for number with an awareness of patterns and relationships;
- variety in the range of methods they employ;
- flexibility in their choice of solutions.

In the approach, attitude to and appreciation of, mathematical challenges they exhibit:
- confidence;
- tenacity;
- creativity;
- attempts to be 'economical' and 'elegant' in reaching their answer.

You may recognise many of these attributes in the most able children you have worked with. It is important to note though that not all able children show themselves to be effective mental calculators. Koshy (2001) highlights that the abilities of gifted mathematicians may not always be reflected in their competence in carrying out mental calculations. They may prefer to identify methods of solutions rather than complete the actual mechanical calculation. However, this description of abilities of an effective mental calculator may provide broad aims towards which *all* the children we teach could aspire. Further, embedded in these characteristics are implications for not only what should be taught but how it could be taught most successfully.

How children learn

Ask a group of adults or children to memorise a specific array of numbers in one minute.
For example:

9	2	7
6	5	4
3	8	1

By comparing and contrasting the methods they use it is possible to identify five distinct approaches. These are:

- physically tracing position of numbers in order as they appear on the grid;
- reciting the numbers;
- holding a mental image,
- re-writing the numbered grid;
- making connections between the order and position of the numbers in relation to a known sequence.

Typically the different ways of learning the numbered grid will match with a single or combination of these approaches. If these particular approaches seem to be chosen when required to memorise information there may be implications for planning for teaching and learning in all aspects of mathematics. So the manner in which teachers present ideas and children are able to respond could embrace the diversity of ways in which children learn. Table 3.3 attempts to exemplify these possibilities.

The obvious implications for the teacher are that planning should provide teaching, learning and assessment opportunities that reflect all of these different methods of learning. The most tangible evidence of this in the classroom is in the use of resources. In both the manner by which the teacher presents ideas and the mode of the children's responses there are a wealth of opportunities to use:

- visual aids (to clarify, stimulate, demonstrate, structure etc...);
- tools to think with (to generate examples to try, rearrange and sort, try out ideas and test theories etc...).

Most primary classrooms in Britain are resourced with number cards, 100 squares, counting sticks, number lines, money, dice and counters. Some choose to use considerably more. In contrast, schools in the Netherlands have policy of using tried and tested resources exclusively. For this reason, their invention, the empty number line, is predominant in the teaching of strategies for mental calculations. So, is there a possibility that planning to include variety in both teaching and learning may be confusing children? Askew (in Askew *et al.* 2001) cautions against the overuse of and dependence on resources. He feels that while they can provide valuable models for clarifying and structuring understanding, ultimately children need to be able to work mentally and independently. I think it is important to understand exactly why a particular teaching and learning approach has been chosen.

Table 3.3   Strategies for teacher presentation and pupil response

Strategy	Example
Doing and moving	**Order a sequence of numbers.** Putting numbers on separate cards allows them to be moved and sorted in positions relative to each other. It also encourages children to develop strategies for making comparisons, i.e. aligning digits on cards in order to match them up in tens, units, tenths etc. . . .
Visualising and contextualising	**Negative numbers.** Children more readily understand and are able to work with negative numbers when they are placed in a familiar context, i.e. money and the notion of debt and credit or the raising or lowering of a lift or temperature gauge.
Listening and talking $30 + 20 = 50$ $35 + 28$ $50 + (10 + 3) = 63$ $8 + 5 = 13$	**Developing strategies for addition.** Requiring children to share resources can encourage discussion. Each pair of children makes two numbers between 10 and 99 with arrow cards. The task is to agree how to find the total of the numbers and to record their method. If one child is responsible for the units and the other the tens, the need to negotiate when the units bridge over the tens emphasises and reinforces the necessary exchange.
Recording and drawing	**Calculating squares of numbers.** The square of 29 is very close to the square of 30 which is 900. The problem arises in knowing what needs to be subtracted. A sketch of both squares is an excellent way of establishing the precise relationship, i.e. $29^2 = 30^2 - 29 - 29 - 1$.
Patterning and relating	**Developing compensation strategies for addition.** 100 squares provide a wealth of possibilities for exploring relationships that help in the development of strategies for calculating. A counter can be placed on any number of the 100 square (most conveniently the top half). By tracking its movement when 0, 1, 10, 20 and then 9 and 19 is added, compensation strategies are illustrated and developed.

For example:

> (i) **A teacher presents addition calculations in a 'real' context, for example, money.**
>
> *Does this context help to give meaning and purpose to the unit of work?*
> *Further, does it help to clarify and support he development of underlying ideas?*
> *Or rather is the context simply 'window dressing' which in fact over-complicates and detracts from the actual learning intended?*

> (ii) **Pupils work individually recording their answers in a table on the worksheet provided.**
>
> *Does recording their work in the table provide a visual display of their answers that will allow children to gain greater insights about addition of numbers (i.e. by identify trends in results)?*
> *Will children have difficulty understanding how to complete the table?*
> *So will this detract from the intended learning? Is the children's recording more about providing evidence of work than supporting the development of learning?*
> *Would allowing the children to work in another way provide greater opportunities for learning (i.e. if the children worked in pairs, choosing how they recorded their results)?*

In every teaching and learning situation critical decisions need to be made:

> **How will the learning intentions be most successfully achieved through the teacher's presentation and the pupils' responses?**

Planning for teaching and learning in mental calculations

In order to offer some ideas about planning for teaching and learning in mental calculations, I have considered each of the components of school mathematics in turn. My ideas are based on my experiences as a teacher, my work with teachers and student teachers and my observations of children in schools.

Teaching and learning facts

Key number bonds (numbers up to 10) and multiplication facts (up to 10×10) need to be memorised. Developing conceptual structures relating to place value and calculations enables children to extend this core of known facts.

- **Understanding**. Although facts are learnt individually, they are more easily learnt if relationships between them are established.

For example:

Using counting sticks to generate tables through repeated addition.

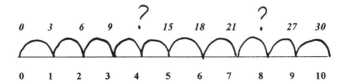

Then removing/concealing facts in order to highlight connections between particular facts.

Figure 3.2

- **Practice**. Regular practice is a vital and ongoing part of learning and extending known facts. It is important to ensure the practice is motivating, purposeful and is appropriate for each child.

For example:

Playing games that allow the practice to be fun as well as 'little and often'.
That challenging, but attainable, targets in terms of speed and accuracy to be set for individuals.

- **Relationships**. Encouraging children to search for links between facts helps them to learn new facts and develop checking strategies if they are uncertain.

For example:

Using known facts to derive new facts helps children to identify patterns in results.

0 5 10 15 20 25 30 35 40 45 50 55 60 65 70 75 80 85 90 95 100

Children can use their knowledge of 10 times table to work out the 5 times table, (i.e. 5 times a number = ½ of 10 times a number).

Illustrating the relationship between the two tables allows valuable checking strategies to be highlighted, (i.e. 5 times any odd number equals an odd answer ending in 5, while 5 times any even number equals an even number ending in 0).

Figure 3.3

- **Versatility**. The value of each fact is increased if it is known and remembered in a number of different forms. This enables groups of facts be more readily applied to as wider range of situations.

For example:

$$3 + 5 = 8$$
$$\text{gives } 5 + 3 = 8$$
$$\text{as well as } 8 - 3 = 5$$
$$\text{and } 8 - 5 = 3$$

Cutting up a particular number fact into five parts provides many opportunities for matching and sorting.

Write 3, +, 5, = and 8 on cards.

On the reverse of the card, write '–' (the inverse operation) and on the reverse of = card, write '≠' (not equal).

This allows children to explore all the possible number sentences that can be created and to decide which ones are not equal.

Figure 3.4

Teaching and learning skills

Accurate use and understanding of the four rules underpins the development of a range of strategies for calculating.

- **Understanding**. Learning experiences need to provide opportunities to gain a broad understanding of each operation and the inter-relationships between them (i.e. subtraction as the inverse of addition and multiplication as repeated addition).

For example:

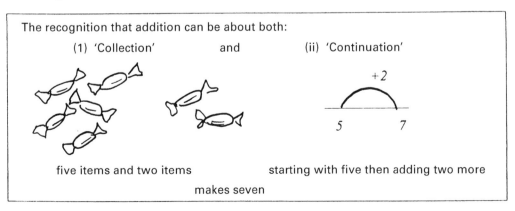

The recognition that addition can be about both:

(1) 'Collection'   and   (ii) 'Continuation'

$+2$

5   7

five items and two items   starting with five then adding two more

makes seven

Figure 3.5

- **Demonstration**. The choice and amount of examples used to demonstrate needs careful consideration.

For example:

> *(i) A decision is necessary to include or exclude potentially ambiguous or difficult examples in early work.*
>
> *Some teachers deliberately 'confront' potential problems, while others prefer to limit the number of difficulties until children have sufficient confidence to tackle them. There does not seem to be significant research to prefer one approach to the other.*

> *(ii) In selecting the number of examples to demonstrate, the needs of both the least and most able need to be balanced.*
>
> *Too many examples can result in a whistle-stop tour explaining the same details over and over again.*
> *Too few patronises those who are quick to grasp ideas.*
> *A solution may lie in matching the number of examples to ensure the understanding of the middle and top groups, allowing for additional time to reinforce ideas with the remaining.*
> *Alternately, I have found children remain engaged in whole-class examples if they are allowed to offer answers using individual white boards.*
> *In this way answers from all the class rather than from one child can be considered.*

- **Competence**. Mastery of skills depends on the quality and not the quantity of practice. It is important that children learn skills correctly initially. Children need to have feedback on their work as soon as possible. Once a child has been allowed to repeat mistakes, these errors can be extremely difficult to 'unlearn'. In my experience children need to repeat a skill at least three and no more than ten times to convince me of their competence.

For example:

> *Providing a selection of questions on individual cards with answers on the back can be an effective way of managing the practice of skills in a mixed ability class.*
>
> *The children need to understand that it is important to get them all correct rather than rush and possibly make mistakes. Having the answers on the back allows children to identify problems immediately. This in turn enables the teacher to focus on those who need the help.*
> *In addition, if questions are categorised in terms of difficulty (i.e. colour coded), children can choose to tackle increasingly more challenging questions as their confidence grows.*

Teaching and learning concepts and conceptual structures

The constructivist theory suggests that children construct their own conceptual structures. A strong understanding of place value and the laws of arithmetic is central to developing mental calculation skills. Alongside quick recall of facts and figuring out skills, children need to develop a conceptual understanding of larger whole numbers, fractional numbers and negative numbers in order to develop their abilities as mental calculators. The more connections children make between different aspects of their learning, the more likely they are to remember what they have learnt, apply it appropriately and grasp new concepts.

- **Experience**. As children's facts and skills develop, they are able to apply their conceptual understanding of place value to derive more facts and increase their skills. The early understanding of '3' extends to include in the meaning of 3 the numbers 30, 300, 0.3 and −3. Similarly, knowing that 3 + 2 = 5 leads to knowing that 300 + 200 = 500 and also that 300 + 2 = 302. While children need a wealth of different learning experiences in order to develop their own conceptual structures, they need to be focused in on what could be learnt.

For example:

Reducing the number of variables in the learning situations that children encounter can help them to focus on the intended learning. In practising long division by repeated addition children could consider either of the following:

(i) ***One particular number is divided in turn by several different numbers***
(i.e. 230 divide by 3, 12, 15 etc. . .):

$$3\overline{)230}$$

The larger the number being divided by, the smaller the answer gets.
So what would heppen if they divided by a very small number?
A number less than one?

(ii) ***A selection of numbers is divided by the same number***
(i.e. 56, 112, 168 etc. . . divided by 15):

$$15\overline{)56}$$

When the same number is divided into larger and larger numbers, the answers should get larger each time.
Do their answers reflect this?
Is there a connection between the first and second answers? Why?

By restricting the number of factors changing in the examples the children tackle, their results can be used to structure and support their thinking.

- **Connections.** Considering how work is presented and how children record their work can help children to identify and make connections.

For example:

Practising doubling in a mental and oral starter can be used to highlight valuable relationships.

Using a number line from 0 to 20 and twelve counters, children are asked to place a counter on the line above the answer as the questions are asked.

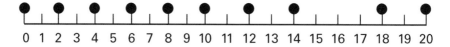

A variety of ways of asking for doubles of numbers from 0 to 10 can be used, (i.e. 7 plus, 2 squared, 2 times 4, double 5 etc. . .)

Include some off the line and one twice (i.e. 2 times 4 and 4 times 2) to invite comments.
Deliberately miss out one double (i.e. double 8) and ask if there is a question they think you should have asked.

By structuring the means by which the children present their answers, the connection between doubles giving even answers is revealed and a visual and numerical connection is made.

Finally the hypothesis that when any number is doubled the answer is even must be tested.
Could they double a number to give the answer 3?

Teaching and learning strategies

Within the skills of addition and subtraction, and multiplication and division, there are a number of key strategies that are employed in particular situations. There are many different taxonomies for these strategies. I will be using the list provided in the QCA (1999) document *The National Numeracy Strategy: Teaching Mental Calculations*. It is important to be familiar with as many of these strategies as possible and to know when it is most appropriate to use them. Children need time and opportunities to select and apply strategies in a variety of situations.

The structures of this experience can differ, (Askew *et al.* 2001) so that:

- specific strategies are taught and then applied in different situations;
- different situations are presented which allow specific strategies to be taught.

Strategies for addition and subtraction

Looking at the strategies identified below there appears to be an order in the level of their sophistication. In fact, if you tracked the introduction and development of each strategy within the National Numeracy Curriculum it quickly becomes apparent that all of the strategies are introduced around Reception and Year 1. Progression in teaching and learning these strategies is through their application. So, for example, 'Counting forwards and backwards' may involve stepping on in ones in the earlier years and in the quarters by Year 6.

Based on work with teachers, students and pupils, each of the following strategies have been exemplified and a range of possible resources for teaching are suggested. For each of the seven strategies there is a set of four questions representing the expectations in level of difficulty increasing across the primary age range. Obviously any number of strategies could be used to calculate any given sum, but there is an implied 'best fit' in the choice of questions.

- **Counting forwards and backwards.** Early ideas about moving backwards and forwards can be established through a variety of number line activities.

For example:

Drop counters in a box.

Ask children to keep track of the running total on their fingers or a numbered curling snake etc...

If nothing is added, no sound is made and the fingers stay still.

When a number is taken out the fingers move back and so on.

Figure 3.6

- **Reordering.** Recognising and using opportunities to re-organise the order in which calculations are carried out is encouraged when children have opportunities to visualise or actually move the numbers involved around.

For example:

> If children generate sums by throwing dice or picking up pairs or strings of numbers on separate cards they have the opportunity to actually choose to place the cards in the order they prefer to work with them.
>
>

Figure 3.7

- **Partitioning – using multiples of 10 and 100.** Children's experiences of constructing and deconstructing numbers with arrow cards (for whole and decimal numbers) supports the development of this strategy most significantly. Asking children to record their methods supports and reveals their thought processes.

For example:

> Using arrow cards to generate sums encourages the idea of considering the most significant numbers first and so on.
>
> Examples that involve the need to exchange from 10s to 100s and so on can be used to raise issues about the suitability of this strategy for particular questions.
>
>

Figure 3.8

- **Partitioning – using bridging through 10.** In order to calculate up or down to a convenient multiple of ten, children need to know the number bonds that make ten. Progression in the use of the strategy depends on a developing understanding of place value.

For example:

> *Number relationships to 10 can be developed playing games with blocks, dice and a strip of paper 10 blocks in length. Children throw dice and collect blocks according to the numbers thrown.*
>
> *When they have a strip of 10 this is a completed tower block and they begin to build another tower.*
>
> *As children build towers they see the blocks they have so far in relation to the amount they need.*
>
> *This helps to establish both visual and numerical relationships in relation to 10.*

- **Partitioning – using near doubles.** Emphasising children's recall of doubles up to 10 and then to 20 gives a starting point to derive doubles of larger and decimal numbers as well as to modify their doubles to consider closely related sets of numbers.

For example:

> Developing strategies for doubling can be supported by using arrow cards to select numbers to double
> (i.e. 43 separates to become 40 and 3 which suggests double 4 and double 3).
>
>
>
> The activity can be reversed to practice halving by working in pairs.
> One child secretly selects 1, 2 or 3 different digit cards to make a number, then works out and writes down the answer.
> The second person halves the number in order to discover the mystery number.

Figure 3.9

- **Partitioning – using compensation.** Early ideas about compensation begin with the modification of known facts to find out something which is closely related. This can be very difficult for some children. A child may work out that 5 + 2 = 7. However, when they are asked what 5 + 3 must be they need to consider the sum as an entirely different question. In my experience, encouraging children to draw the question and then to modify this drawing by adding another one (changing the two items to a three) can help. Similarly, ways of illustrating and representing can help children to understand the notion of compensation more fully.

For example:

> 100 squares can be used to plot the visual, spatial and numerical effects of adding and subtracting (i.e. +0, +2, +10, +20, –0, –2, –10 etc. . .)
>
> These ideas can be extended to explore the addition and subtraction amounts which are closely
> related to these.
> So +9 is seen as +10 – 1;
> Similarly –19 as –20 + 1 etc. . .

Figure 3.10

- **Partitioning – using bridging through numbers other than 10.** Similar to the strategy of bridging through 10, children need to develop experience and confidence in numbers.

For example:

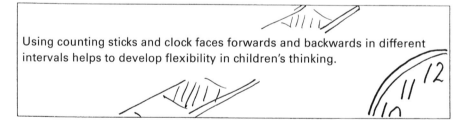

Using counting sticks and clock faces forwards and backwards in different intervals helps to develop flexibility in children's thinking.

Figure 3.11

Strategies for multiplication and division

Children's development and memorisation of multiplication facts up to 10 × 10 is essential for the development of effective strategies for multiplication and division. If children are able to generate these facts and practise them in a variety of ways, they are more likely to remember and be able to apply their learning. Using their developing understanding of place value and the laws of mathematics, children can use each single known fact to derive many other facts.

- **Knowing multiplication and division facts and using these to derive related facts**.

If 5 × 9 = 45

(a) 9 × 5 = 45

(b) 45 ÷ 5 = 9

(c) 45 ÷ 9 = 5

Figure 3.12

As mentioned earlier, these related facts can be generated by separating each part of the multiplication fact onto cards that can then be rearranged.

For example:

Write 5, 9 and 45, then ÷ and × on either side of a card and similarly = and ≠ on another card.

Using either side of the cards children can rearrange the sets of cards.

Statements that are equal and are not equal can be formed.

Figure 3.13

- **Multiplying and dividing by multiples of 10 with whole and decimals numbers**. Encouraging estimation supports these strategies. If children are given answers they can be challenged to speculate on possible questions.

For example:

If 5 × 9 = 45, what multiplication fact could give 45,000?

- **Doubling and halving involving larger numbers and fractions**. Doubling and halving can be most efficient calculation strategies. It is often quicker and reliable to double and double again rather than multiply by 4. Challenging children to use only a specified group of calculations can help them to recognise the versatility and potential of doubling and halving.

For example:

Try to multiply by 42 each of the following numbers in turn: 12, 24 and 15.

Only allow children to use the operations + and − , × 10 and halving or doubling. NB: By multiplying the same number '42' each time the focus of the children's thinking is on finding strategies for multiplying by 12, 24 and 15.

- **Multiplying and dividing by single-digit numbers and two-digit numbers**: *Using (i) factors, (ii) partitioning and (iii) closely related facts.*

(i) Factors

(a) $5 \times 9 = 5 \times (3 \times 3)$ *split into factors which gives* $15 \times 3 = 45;$
(b) $25 \times 36 = (5 \times 5) \times (2 \times 2 \times 3 \times 3),$ *reordered becomes* $(5 \times 2) \times (5 \times 2)$
$\times \quad (3 \times 3),$ *which gives* $10 \times 10 \times 9 = 900;$
(c) $450 - 18 = 450 - (2 \times 3 \times 3),$ *expressing 18 as a product of prime factors and in small steps* $450 - 2 = 225,$ *then* $225 - 3 = 75,$ *finally* $75 - 3 = 25.$

This strategy is rather neglected, but has the potential to reduce the need for larger and potentially more difficult calculations. It relies on children's familiarity of numbers as product of different combinations of their factors.

So 24 is equal to (4×6) *or* $(2 \times 2 \times 2 \times 3).$

Many practical activities support the development of this understanding.

(ii) Partitioning

(a) *If you did not know your 5 times tables you could partition 5 into 'bits', so that*
$5 \times 9 = (2 + 3) \times 9.$
Using the distributive law $(2 + 3) \times 9 = (2 \times 9) + (3 \times 9);$
(b) *Similarly if you had forgotten your 9 times table you could partition 9 in relation to 10, a table you could recall.*
So $5 \times 9 = 5 \times (10 - 1),$ *again using the distributive law* $5 \times (10 - 1) = (5 \times 10) - (5 \times 1),$ *and* $50 - 5 = 45.$

More usually numbers are partitioned into multiples of 10, in order to structure successive multiplications with one-, two- and three-digit numbers. The favoured way for teaching and learning these methods is with arrow cards and the 'grid' method of multiplication.

For example:

When 25 × 18 is considered, arrow cards can be used to reinforce the structure of each number.

If the numbers involved are used to sketch a rectangle (possibly to scale on squared paper initially) the question is much more easily understood and calculated.

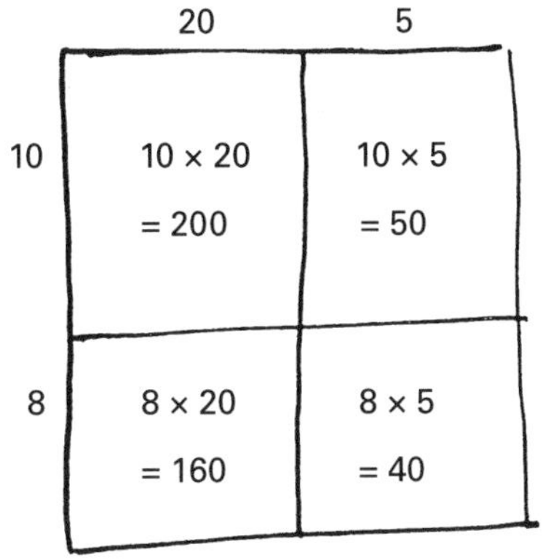

	20	5
10	10 × 20 = 200	10 × 5 = 50
8	8 × 20 = 160	8 × 5 = 40

In this way 25 × 18 = 200 + 160 + 50 + 40, which gives an answer of 450.

Figure 3.14

(iii) Closely related facts

This is a sophisticated strategy with enormous potential. However, children need first to be able to identify related facts which could be of assistance in calculating and to remember to make the appropriate modification to arrive at the correct answer. Drawing can help children to make relevant connections and understand the required adjustment to be made.

For example:

(a) If you could not remember your 9 times table, you can use other related facts that you can remember and adjust the answer as required.

So 5 × 9 is nearly 5 × 10 = 50.

But 9 not 10 lots of 5 are required.

So the 50 needs to be reduced by 5.

This gives 50 – 5 = 45.

(b) This understanding can be extended to consider any number of related multiplications:

$$42 \times 9 = 42 \times 10 - (1 \times 42);$$
$$42 \times 8 = 42 \times 10 - (2 \times 42);$$
$$42 \times 11 = 42 \times 10 + (1 \times 42);$$
$$42 \times 99 = 42 \times 100 - (1 \times 42) \text{ and so on ...}$$

Figure 3.15

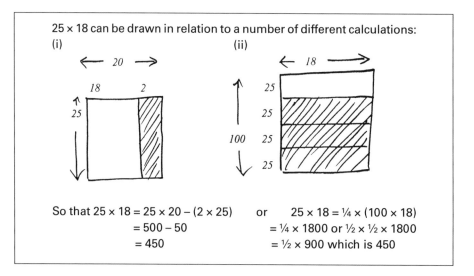

25 × 18 can be drawn in relation to a number of different calculations:

(i)   (ii)

So that 25 × 18 = 25 × 20 – (2 × 25)   or   25 × 18 = ¼ × (100 × 18)
                = 500 – 50   = ¼ × 1800 or ½ × ½ × 1800
                = 450   = ½ × 900 which is 450

Figure 3.16

Teaching and learning approaches and attitudes to mathematics

Part of being a mental calculator is being both quick and accurate in reaching the answer. As has been discussed, ideas about learning the required facts, skills, conceptual structure and strategies may each be involved in some measure of direct teaching. Acquiring positive feelings about mathematics, along with flexible and inventive ways of working, are vital to becoming an effective mental calculator. However, children's development may rely more on indirect than direct teaching (Ernest 2000), i.e. it will be through the learning environment established by the teacher, through their own attitudes and appreciation of mathematics, the teaching and learning opportunities they provide as well as the expectation for learning they set. Teaching and learning that consistently focus on such ways of working may be unhelpful in achieving this goal. With pressure on the time allowed and the necessity to give the correct answer, there is little incentive to take a 'risk' and try something new.

- **Role model**. Teacher's personal confidence, interest and even enthusiasm for mathematics is at the heart of the learning environment they create.

For example:

> *The increase in the use of interactive teaching methods and the provision of a variety of resources to work with has helped to portray teachers as being very 'involved' in mathematics.*

- **Teaching and learning experiences**. Teaching and learning needs to embrace the breadth of mathematics and include opportunities to learn through a variety of approaches.

For example:

> *(i) If tasks are more open and longer, encourage discussion and most significantly focus on the choice of 'journey' rather than the 'destination'. Children are then less likely to default to the safe and tested methods.*
> *(ii) Activities need to be motivating, interesting and purposeful to engage and hold children's attention and sustain their concentration.*

- **Expectations**. When children are aware that their goal for learning is the aspiration for mathematical 'elegance', expectations can be more about process than product. The self-belief and confidence to develop ideas is based on personal achievement and success.

For example:

> (i) *If the focus of work is on quality rather than quantity, children may be encouraged to be more creative and adventurous in their work.*

> (ii) *The difficulty of the tasks must match the ability of each child and represent a personal, but attainable challenge.*
> *This challenge might be in terms of size of number, types of operation, combination of operations, complexity or number of steps, accuracy, speed, choice of strategy etc...*

Summary

The teaching of mental calculation has been debated for decades. The Cockroft Report (1982) identified the development of effective mental strategies, together with opportunities to engage in practical work and discussion about mathematical ideas, as crucial to the most successful teaching and learning. Most recently, the implementation of the National Numeracy Strategy in schools has placed the development of mental calculations centrally within the mathematics curriculum. It may be helpful to consider the reasons for teaching mental calculations in terms of effects on attitudes to and learning in mathematics and for its own sake.

Effects on attitudes to and learning in mathematics

From a teacher and pupil perspective the impact of changes in the primary mathematics classroom were positive and rapid. Koshy (2000) found that both teachers and pupils enjoyed mental mathematics lessons that were delivered with enthusiasm and imagination. There may be a number of factors that have brought about the improvements in attitudes to teaching and learning mathematics. The clarity of planning and support provided by both the National Numeracy Framework and the three-part daily mathematics lesson seem to be the most significant reasons. The majority of teachers speedily and successfully adapted to quite dramatic changes to many aspects of their previous practices. This cycle of change continues to evolve as pupils enjoy and benefit from more interactive teaching and an increase in the use of resources. Within weeks of the introduction of the strategy, teachers were enthusiastic about the impact on their pupils' learning and attitudes in mental calculations. So significant were these improvements that some parents with children of different ages noted anomalies in their comparative progress. For example, while a pupil in Year 6 struggled to adapt from traditional taught methods, the younger sibling showed confidence in learning new mental strategies. This 'catch-up' situation has been more recently noted in study of children in their transition to secondary school (Lenga and Ogden 2000).

Mental calculations for their own sake

Being effective at carrying out mental calculations seems to give greater confidence and aptitude across the mathematics curriculum. Indeed, there is a growing importance in the procedures and processes for their own sake. Engaging in the manipulation of numbers involved in mental mathematics develops an understanding of number structures and relationships as well as creative thinking and problem-solving skills. Research in Australia, (Reys 1992) highlights the growing importance in schools of procedures and processes in their own right. There is the belief that teaching mental calculations supports children's learning in all aspects of the mathematics curriculum, contributing to:

- deeper understanding of number structures and properties;
- more creative and independent thinking: using their understanding to develop ingenious ways of manipulating numbers;
- skills and strategies associated with problem solving and computational estimation.

Implications for teaching mental calculations

This chapter began by attempting to distinguish mental calculations from other aspects of school mathematics. A personal view of what should be taught and how it is most effectively learnt has been given in order to reveal more about the nature of mental calculation. It has been established that mental arithmetic, written and mental calculations require the speedy recall of facts and accurate application of skills. The external responses from a child engaged in all numerical activities may be the same: a single correct answer. However, I believe that it is the *internal responses* that children make that distinguish them as being engaged in mental calculations.

Becoming an effective mental calculator involves learning in all aspects of school mathematics. It therefore necessitates teaching that is not just about exposition and practice. Planning should provide opportunities for children to develop, refine and extend their thinking skills through discussion, practical work, problem solving and investigative work if they are to fully realise their potential as mental calculators.

Since the introduction of the National Numeracy Strategy, schools, teachers and pupils have been saturated with new ideas, teaching materials, different ways of working and changing expectations. There is now a wealth of advice and resources readily available to teachers. Yet no matter how accessible these may seem:

(i) How realistic is it for teachers to effectively search, select and assimilate and then put these ideas and resources into action in the classroom?

(ii) With the ever-increasing and changing demands placed on teachers in every aspect of their work, is there, logistically, the opportunity for them to critically appraise and reflect on their own practice?

Without the time and working environment to research, review and discuss ideas with colleagues, it may seem an impossible task for teachers to effectively teach mental calculations. Planning to teach mental calculation depends on establishing balance in teaching and learning experiences. It involves considering the planned learning intentions and making judgements about the:

- method of *teacher presentation* that will give clarity and purpose;
- mode of *pupil response* that is manageable and contributes to their understanding;
- specific *resources* that provide *visual clues* and *tools to think with;*
- nature of the *mathematical activity* in which the children will be engaged;
- opportunities for the: (i) *introduction and teaching of areas of new learning*, (ii) *practice and refinement of learning*, (iii) *application and extension of understanding;*
- ways in which *progression* in children's learning will be ensured and monitored.

In this chapter I have been able to reflect on my own experiences in order to offer suggestions for the teaching and learning of mental calculations. I hope that the ideas considered make a small contribution towards supporting teachers in their planning. Their usefulness really depends on teachers being afforded the time and opportunity to use them in order to evolve their own personal philosophy for teaching mental calculations.

Acknowledgements

Love and thanks to my husband Paul, children Robert and Helen and my parents for their help and patience. Many thanks also to Graham Marinner and all the teachers and staff at Archdeacon Cambridge Primary School, Twickenham, with particular thanks to Etaine Gibson, Bernadette Game and Judy Holt for our enthusiastic discussions about mathematics teaching. Particular thanks to Valsa Koshy for her support and advice.

References

Askew, M., Robinson, D. and Mosley, F. (2001) *Teaching Mental Strategies: Number Calculations in Years 5 and 6*. London: Beam Education.

Cockcroft, W. H. (1982) *Mathematics Counts: Report of the Committee of Inquiry into the Teaching of Mathematics in Schools*. London: HMSO.

Ernest, P. (2000) 'Teaching and Learning Mathematics', in Koshy, V., Ernest, P. and Casey, R. (eds) *Mathematics for Primary Teachers*. London: Routledge.

Koshy, V. (2000) *Effective Teaching in Numeracy for the National Mathematics Framework*. London: Hodder and Stoughton.

Koshy, V. (2001) *Teaching Mathematics to Able Children*. London: David Fulton Publishers.

Lenga, R. and Ogden, V. (2000) 'Lost in Transit: Attainment deficit in pupil transition from Key Stage 2 to Key Stage 3', *Viewpoint* 13. London: Institute of Education.

QCA (1999) *The National Numeracy Strategy: Teaching Mental Calculations*. London: QCA Publications.

Reys, R. (1992) 'Mental Computation: Some ideas for teachers and directions for teaching', in Irons, C. J. (ed) *Challenging Children to Think when they Compute*. Brisbane: The Centre for Mathematics and Science Education.

Thompson, I. (1999) 'Mental Calculation Strategies for Addition and Subtraction, Part 1', *Mathematics in Schools* 28(5), November. Mathematics Association.

CHAPTER 4

Making human sense of it: contexts for using ICT to enhance the teaching of numeracy

JOHN GARVEY

Introduction

The rising use of the Internet has highlighted the fact that not only do we have to adjust to the world around us, but that there is also a virtual world that needs to be organised and understood if we are to make sense of the 'age of information'. In Margaret Donaldson's (1978) terms, we need to 'make human sense of it'. A key element of responding appropriately to this challenge is the need to develop in children a range of information handling skills. Within schools, Frawley (1992:19) has commented that 'the handling of information is a pre-requisite of virtually every area of the National Curriculum.' Such a view is complemented by Straker and Govier's (1996:36) assertion that 'being able to deduce information from a graphical display, to interpret what it means and to offer some explanations for it, are skills which are becoming increasingly important across the whole curriculum.' This chapter will investigate good classroom practice and from this identify strategies for enabling children to make progress in developing key aspects of mathematical understanding and in particular, information handling, through the judicious use of ICT. There will be particular emphasis on progression in the use of open-ended applications such as databases and spreadsheets and to a lesser extent on Logo and programmable robots.

Key Stage 1: collecting, representing and understanding data using databases

Farmer Giles' problem

Consider the following Year 1 play situation that was used by the teacher to develop an introduction to data handling. With reference to a toy farm that children had been playing with, the teacher explained that Farmer Giles needed to move his animals indoors for the winter – the cows would need to go into one shed, sheep into another, as would the pigs and ducks. The farmer wanted to count his animals to see how much food would be needed for the winter for each group of animals. Through whole-class discussion, children came up with a range of ideas, but the one agreed upon was that, if the animals were lined up, they could easily be counted. Groups of children were then encouraged to line up groups of animals and count them (in the process developing their understanding of sets and number). To complement this, they were introduced to a simple data handling program 'Counting Pictures'. The toy farmyard was placed next to the computer and children were encouraged to use the computer mouse to 'count' the animals lined up in the farmyard – with each click of the mouse, the number of animals on screen in each column increased by one. In this way children were able to represent real objects pictorially on screen by 'telling' the computer via the mouse. Additionally, at the click of a mouse, the children proved able to explore different representations of the same data – animal pictures could be represented by coloured squares. The teacher followed up this work by printing out copes of graphs drawn by the computer and posing a range of open-ended and closed questions for children to respond to:

- what does the graph tell us?
- tell me three things about the columns of animals
- how many cows are there?
- how many more cows are there than ducks?
- how many animals are there altogether?
- could we organise the animals in a different way?

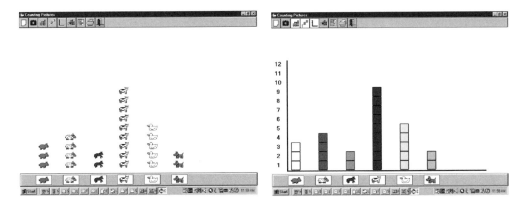

Figure 4.1   Farm animals – pictorial and symbolic graphical representation

Such work is based upon The National Numeracy Strategy (DfEE 1999) Teaching Programme for Year One, where children are expected to 'solve a given problem by sorting, classifying and organising information in simple ways, such as using objects and pictures' and to 'discuss and explain results'. Appropriate teacher questioning was critical in helping children to organise data into a form that was meaningful to them – in other words, to turn data into information.

Cuddly's picnic

This distinction between data and information was built upon by another Year 1 teacher in a context which was interesting and relevant to the children – that of a cuddly's (cuddly toy) picnic. The teacher told her children that a picnic was to be organised for the children's teddy bears or cuddlies, explaining that, in order to make the trip a success, some planning was necessary. This was introduced through a whole-class carpet session, drawing upon the principle of enabling children to identify the needs of others. The first step was for children to bring in their own cuddlies to help to personalise any choices they would make. Children were asked what the cuddlies would need for their picnic. Responses varied from food and drink, to umbrellas and a tablecloth. One useful category of need identified by the children was that of sandwiches. The teacher then asked each child for their cuddly's sandwich preference and then let them place their soft toy in a single undifferentiated central pile. The teacher asked the children to identify the sandwich that each teddy wanted. The children found this impossible, as the pile of data (cuddlies) they were confronted with did not yield any useful information (organised data). Through open-ended questioning the teacher was able to elicit from children a way of organising the data into a form which would enable them to make decisions about the number and type of sandwiches needed. Those children familiar with the idea of organising objects into sets and lining up suggested that they could place the teddies in lines, which the teacher supplemented with real jars of jam, peanut butter and pieces of cheese to label each column. Further work was done in organising the cuddlies into sets in different ways based on the use of Venn diagrams to display sandwich preferences which would overlap two sets (e.g. a cuddly who wanted a cheese and ham sandwich).

At this point the teacher introduced children to the data-handling program, 'Counter'. This allows children to type in data in columns and then allows that data to be converted into graphical form. The children were told that they could use the computer to store lots of data and present it in ways that would help them to plan for and answer questions about their picnic. Printouts from the graphs derived from Counter were used as a focus for teacher questioning. Children also used the printouts to show the sandwich makers (parents) the range of sandwiches needed for the picnic. The children were then asked about which graph the parents found most useful in helping them to decide the number of sandwiches needed for the picnic. They reported that parents found the bar chart easier to use as the pie charts gave no indication of the number of sandwiches in each category.

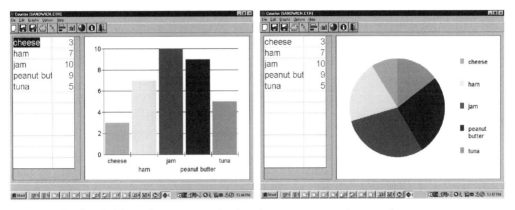

Figure 4.2   Sandwich preferences – selecting the most appropriate graph

The teacher commented that the children were developing a variety of data handling skills:

- organising data into information in a real context;
- understanding the need to give the computer accurate information;
- organising and representing data in different but meaningful ways;
- realising that a computer can help in storing data and presenting it in different ways at the click of a mouse;
- discovering that some ways of representing information are more useful than others.

Bruner (1957, 1971) stressed the vital role of the adult or 'experienced other' in supporting and extending children's developing understanding of the world around them, characterising intelligence as the ability to 'go beyond the information given.' Through questioning, work with real objects and the judicious use of ICT, the teacher helped children to develop and express their understanding at different levels. Bruner distinguished between three modes in which knowledge is expressed or represented – Enactive, Iconic and Symbolic. The data handling work here exemplifies these modes. The Enactive mode is defined by action and practical activity – in this case, by children physically organising the animals and cuddlies into different categories and (in the case of sandwich preferences) labelling those categories with real objects. ICT was used to support the development of the Iconic or pictorial representation of categories – the value of different forms of Iconic representation was explored though open-ended questioning by the teacher using the computer printouts of graphs. The database also proved valuable in enabling children to see the way in which symbols (squares in this case) could be used to represent pictures in the graphical representation of animals, thus supporting children in understanding that data can be represented symbolically. Wood (1990) makes the point that Bruner's conception of 'knowledge representation is that the representation created must bear a one-to-one correspondence with the event or activity that it depicts' (p. 183). The instantaneous manner in which the categories could be represented in Iconic or Symbolic mode on screen was of real value in helping children to see the correspondence between different ways of representing mathematical knowledge.

Such progression in data handling also exemplifies Bruner's concept of the 'Spiral Curriculum' where concepts are revisited at increasingly more complex levels of sophistication. As Bruner (1966) claimed, 'any subject can be taught effectively in some intellectually honest form to any child at any stage of development' (p. 27). Two student teachers (Trier 1999, Lawrence 1999) accepted the challenge laid down by Bruner in their work on data handling with a Year 1 class. They were keen to find a way for children to develop their own personal records, incorporating a small range of field names (headings), with a view to exploring data-handling using a card-index type database (First Workshop). They enabled children to record data about themselves pictorially and symbolically by developing a card for each child.

Figure 4.3   Card-index style record for datafile

From these cards one can see that Bethan is aged four, with blue eyes, size nine feet, blond hair and likes beans on toast. The students entered the children's records into the database and with support, children were able to identify their own records in the datafile and derive simple graphs from the data. The graphs were displayed and used as a basis for simple open-ended questioning by the students.

An interesting twist on the concept of the Spiral Curriculum was observed in teacher use of the graphical data on sandwich preferences. While a Year 6 class was lined up for assembly, their attention was drawn to the graphs in Figure 4.2, which were prominently displayed in the corridor next to the school hall. The teacher posed the following questions and followed them up in class based sessions:

- what is the difference between the columns?
- what is the mode?
- what is the mean?
- what is the median?
- estimate the percentage of children who prefer cheese sandwiches.

Questioning strategies such as these demonstrate that the simplest of graphical representations can be used to challenge children's thinking about and understanding of mathematical terms, in relation to the National Numeracy Strategy (*op. cit.*) guidelines for organising and interpreting data.

Key Stage 2: organising and interpreting data using databases

The principles of using the computer in involving contexts to represent data in different ways was continued with Key Stage 2 children, who were taught to enter data into a more advanced card-index type database and encouraged to use the database to support the interpretation of data and the solving of problems. One context investigated with Year 6 children was that of Giants, stimulated by class reading of *The Iron Man* by Ted Hughes in the Literacy Hour. The teacher decided to use this as the context for some problem-solving work, using the database Information Workshop. Drawing upon an idea gleaned from the National Council for Education's *Making Sense of Information* (1997), the teacher contrived a situation where giant footprints and handprints had been found in the school ground. She challenged the children to estimate the height of the visitor so that they could assess the risk he or she might pose. The teacher invited children to come up with hypotheses concerning any relationships between the lengths of various parts of the body. The following hypotheses were generated:

- the taller someone is, the heavier they are;
- the longer their foot size, the taller they would be;
- the longer their handspan, the taller they would be;
- the longer their reach (distance across the shoulder from fingertip to fingertip) the taller they would be.

Initially children were invited to measure parts of their own bodies to investigate any links between them. A mass of data was collected on handspans, reach, foot length, height and weight. Children set about investigating whether there were any relationships between the length of body parts, but found the process somewhat long-winded and laborious. At this point the teacher intervened and discussed ways forward with the whole class, guiding them into the possibility of using a database to ease the process of representing data in different ways. A datafile was developed, based on the measurements collected, with a view to organising the data and investigating it in depth.

Children were encouraged to investigate different ways of representing the data to see if any particular means would be of real value in exploring relationships between variables such as height, reach, weight, foot size and handspan. It was found that they had real problems with this and needed to be heavily guided by the teacher in the direction of using scattergraphs to explore the relationship between numerical values. The teacher found that the most effective way of scaffolding understanding of the representation of data on a scattergram was to plot a single child's reach and height on to a large-scale pair of axes, using paper and pencil. A collection of measurements was added to the graph so that children could see a pattern emerging. At this point children were guided to exploring scattergraphs on the computer. The value of this was that they could move between exploring the comparison of different variables very quickly and thus test hypotheses they had made, without resorting to what would have been perceived as cumbersome pencil and paper methods. The teacher found that the most effective way of ensuring that children could interpret scattergraphs correctly was by inserting incorrect data on to a printout using an OHP transparency and inviting children to comment on the data (an interactive whiteboard or LCD projector would have been invaluable here).

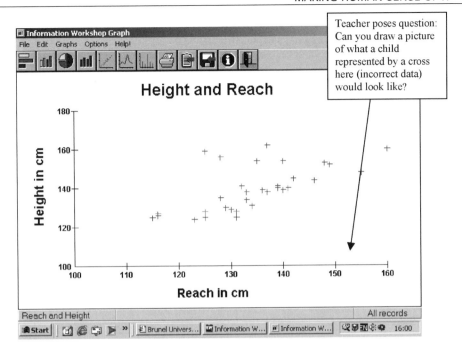

Figure 4.4   Scattergraph of reach and height

Time constraints did not allow the teacher to explore the giant investigation using a spreadsheet, which would have afforded an alternative approach to exploring and testing hypotheses involving numbers.

Spreadsheets

The Key Stage 2 investigation above could have been explored with a spreadsheet as the main data handling tool. Spreadsheets also have great potential as a tool for modelling mathematical situations. Large numbers can be manipulated easily and repeated calculations can be explored with a view to identifying patterns within number investigations. A major problem is finding situations that require the need for simple formulae at a level that children will understand. Cross-curricular work can be fruitful in this regard. Take the case of evaluating products in design and technology. In this case Year 4 children were evaluating a range of fruit salads, including one they had made themselves. They were guided in the development of formulae and graphs by the teacher as part of a whole-class ICT session.

The benefit of introducing children to the construction of a table such as this is that it can be used as a template in a variety of investigations across the curriculum. In a subsequent design and technology investigation into carrier bags, the children were able to independently use a similar table to record their evaluations of the strengths of a variety of carrier bags. Similarly the template for the

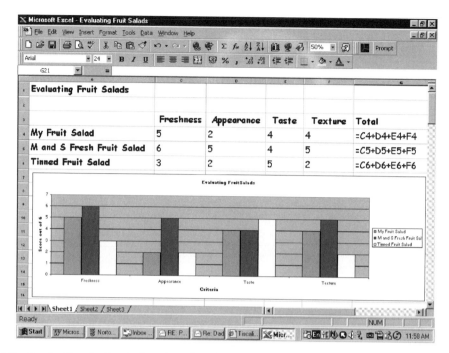

Fig 4.5   Evaluating fruit salads using simple formulae and graphing within a spreadsheet

table used here proved useful in a range of science investigations including the testing of durability of a range of fabrics and the varying speeds of cars travelling down ramps at different angles. Through such investigations children can be led to an understanding of the value of mathematics and ICT applications in genuinely involving contexts.

During the Numeracy Hour, a Year 5 teacher was investigating mental maths problems based upon such statements as 'I think of a number, double it and take away 2'. As part of work on algebra, she incorporated such problems into the main teaching sessions involving the use of pencil and paper methods. She employed the strategy of making the problems increasingly long-winded. When signs of boredom and exasperation started to surface, she introduced the idea of using a spreadsheet to ease the process of number crunching. Introducing spreadsheets to children can be a daunting process for teachers as the cell interface presented on screen can seem far from user-friendly and there is significant potential for children getting confused about the construction of formulae. Bearing this in mind, the teacher employed an approach which has a strong tradition within the teaching of mathematics, but which has been formalised as an integral part of the National Curriculum for Design and Technology – that of focused tasks. A focused task is one which enables children to develop and practise skills as a precursor to using that skill to solve a problem. Using the school computer suite, the teacher introduced the children to the use of increasingly sophisticated formulae on a column by column basis:

(1) I think of a number;
(2) I add 6 to that number (first operation);
(3) I multiply that number by 4 (second operation);
(4) I take away the number I first thought of (result);
(5) What is the number I started with?

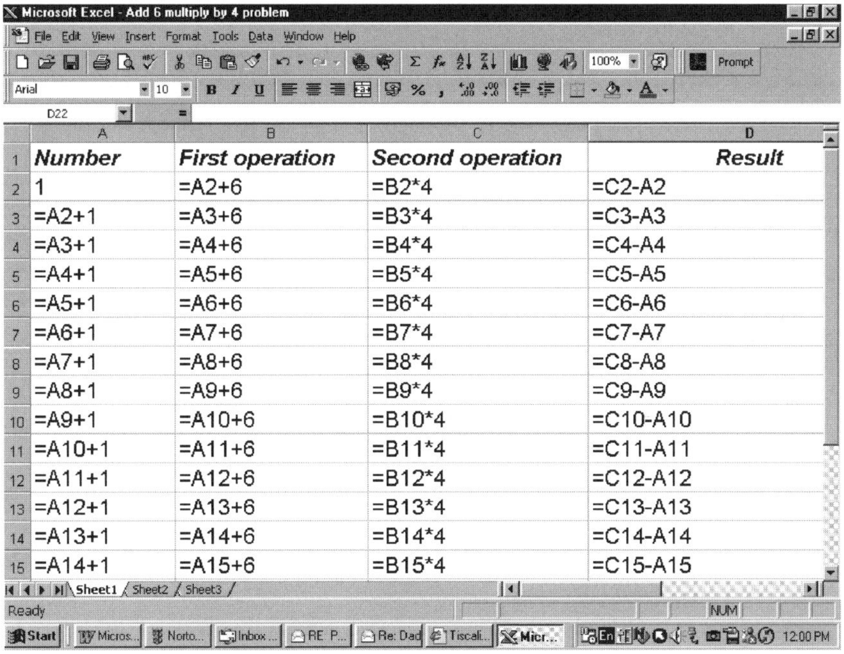

	A	B	C	D
	Number	First operation	Second operation	Result
1	1	=A2+6	=B2*4	=C2-A2
2	=A2+1	=A3+6	=B3*4	=C3-A3
3	=A3+1	=A4+6	=B4*4	=C4-A4
4	=A4+1	=A5+6	=B5*4	=C5-A5
5	=A5+1	=A6+6	=B6*4	=C6-A6
6	=A6+1	=A7+6	=B7*4	=C7-A7
7	=A7+1	=A8+6	=B8*4	=C8-A8
8	=A8+1	=A9+6	=B9*4	=C9-A9
9	=A9+1	=A10+6	=B10*4	=C10-A10
10	=A10+1	=A11+6	=B11*4	=C11-A11
11	=A11+1	=A12+6	=B12*4	=C12-A12
12	=A12+1	=A13+6	=B13*4	=C13-A13
13	=A13+1	=A14+6	=B14*4	=C14-A14
14	=A14+1	=A15+6	=B15*4	=C15-A15

Figure 4.6   Using formulae in a spreadsheet

The focused task approach involved breaking down the problem into small steps. The activity lent itself well to differentiating work by the adjustment of the complexity of the formulae presented to children. Such work can be of great benefit in allowing children to investigate number patterns in a relatively pain-less manner and as an introduction to the use of symbols (cell references) in formulae. When children were reasonably confident in using simple formulae, the teacher invited them to comment on the advantages of using the spreadsheet. The most pertinent comments ranged from, 'it's fun to highlight the numbers and drag them down and watch the numbers come up,' to, 'after you put the formula in, the computer does the work for you.'

In the following year the teacher involved children in a survey of pocket money. They were then invited to make a choice between the following arrangements. They could either accept over a six month period:

(1) £2 a week *or*

(2)   1p for the first week, 2p in the second week, 4p in the third week, 8p in the third week etc.

The majority children initially opted for the first option, estimating that this would yield the most cash. They were then challenged to work out whether they had made the correct choice, with some preliminary work done with paper and pencil. Most children could quickly see that they had made the wrong choice. To ease the process of repeated multiplication, children were then allowed to use calculators and guided in the use of formulae within spreadsheets. Calculators proved effective in this regard, with children surprised at the exponential growth of wealth in the second option. However, the visual nature of the growth of numbers within the spreadsheets proved to be captivating – the prospect of receiving over £300,000 a week after six months led some to comment that they would try to secure such a deal with their own parents.

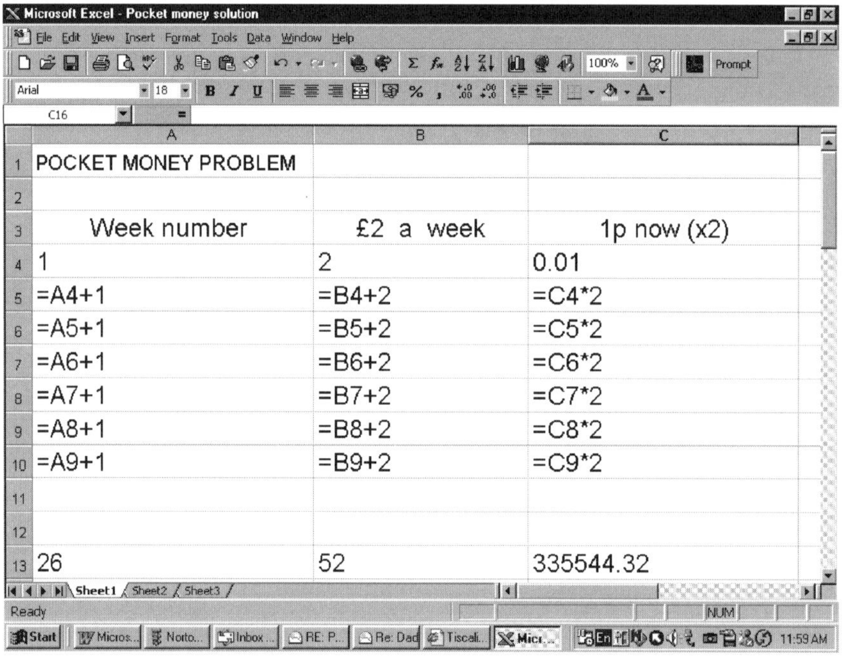

	A	B	C
1	POCKET MONEY PROBLEM		
2			
3	Week number	£2 a week	1p now (x2)
4	1	2	0.01
5	=A4+1	=B4+2	=C4*2
6	=A5+1	=B5+2	=C5*2
7	=A6+1	=B6+2	=C6*2
8	=A7+1	=B7+2	=C7*2
9	=A8+1	=B8+2	=C8*2
10	=A9+1	=B9+2	=C9*2
11			
12			
13	26	52	335544.32

Figure 4.7   Pocket money problem

The principle of an involving context, appropriate scaffolding of the task by the teacher and using the computer to ease the process of calculation proved to be of genuine benefit in exploring how numbers can surprise and inform. The National Numeracy Strategy (*op. cit.*) recommends such approaches to work in mathematics:

Where teaching is concerned, better numeracy standards occur when teachers:

- devote a high proportion of lesson time to direct teaching of whole classes and groups, making judicious use of resources such as ICT to support teaching, not replace it;
- use and give pupils access to resources, including ICT, to model mathematical ideas and methods.

(www.standards.gov.uk.numeracy)

Logo and programmable robots

Seymour Papert's (1982,1993) espousal of his programming language Logo and associated programmable robots as 'objects to think with' has genuine resonance for teachers and children alike. Straker (in Straker and Govier 1996) has suggested that children begin to 'program' (plan a sequence of actions) when they are very young, for example, when they are planning the sequence of moves in a game. The use of programmable robots can be very beneficial for young children, as they have the potential to be 'body syntonic' (Ainley 1996), enabling children to relate the movement of the robot to their own bodies, allowing them to take ownership of the control of the robot as a precursor for more formal programming with Logo. Logo also has the potential to enable children to understand and develop ways of representing their understanding of mathematical concepts such as estimation, shape, space, direction and angle. The following work by a student teacher (Parry 2000) with Year 1 children illuminates this. She chose to use Pixie – a small programmable robot with a simple keyboard which allows children to select distances and left or right turns – to investigate concepts of number, direction and programming. The robot was changed into an aeroplane and children were challenged to 'fly' it from house to house across a world map. Initially children were happy to work on a trial and error basis in Enactive mode, commanding the robot to move from house to house. When challenged to 'fly the route in one go' the children decided, through discussion, that drawing a map of the route would be useful – representing information in Iconic mode. More able children in the class were able to internalise and represent the route the aeroplane would take in a symbolic manner.

A major benefit of programmable robots is their potential for enabling cooperation between children in the solving of problems and the opportunity they afford for children to talk about mathematics. Consider the following interaction, where children were prompted by the student teacher to demonstrate their emerging understanding about number, direction and programming:

Teacher: Pixie almost got there. What instructions will need to be changed?
Imogen: She has to take the end one off *(indicating that the last instruction has to be changed)*.
Gagondeep: Yes and put another forward one on instead.
Caitlin: No, I need to do six of them *(forward)* because I didn't actually make it there.
Teacher: So then what do you want to do?
Caitlin: Then I want to go that way.
Teacher: Right?
Caitlin: Yes, right and then after right, then that way. Up one and then that way.

Figure 4.8   Programmable robots – pictorial and symbolic representation

Such work with young children on programmable robots is critical in enabling them to develop sophistication at a later stage in using Logo as a programming tool, allowing them to break down complex problems into sub tasks, viewing mistakes not as disastrous, but as an integral part of the learning process. Work with Logo has the added potential of allowing children to enter 'microworlds' (Papert 1982), where they can explore concepts of shape, space, and angle in challenging and rich contexts.

Conclusion

The work of Donaldson (*op. cit.*) stressed that children operate best within contexts that they can relate to and understand. The descriptions of teachers' work in this chapter demonstrate how dedicated professionals with a keen understanding of the potential of ICT have provided children with contexts where they can develop skills of representing, organising and interpreting information with a view to deepening their understanding of the world around them. Central to teaching and learning were strategies such as the appropriate use of open-ended and closed questions, the planning of practical activities embedded within tasks involving the use of ICT and the conscious encouragement of different modes of representing information. The range of contexts investigated here is not intended to be definitive. With the current highly prescriptive primary curriculum it is essential for teachers to exercise their imagination in designing contexts to extend the boundaries of children's thinking and understanding of mathematical concepts, complemented and informed by the judicious use of ICT.

References

Ainley, J. (1996) *Enriching Primary Mathematics with I.T.* London: Hodder and Stoughton.

Bruner, J. S. (1957) Going Beyond the Information Given. Reprinted in *Beyond the Information Given* (Ed. Anglin, J. M .1973). New York: W. W. Norton and Co.

Bruner, J. S. (1966) *Towards a Theory of Instruction.* Cambridge, Mass: Harvard University Press.

Bruner, J. S. (1971) *The Relevance of Education.* New York: W. W. Norton and Co.

Donaldson, M. (1978) *Children's Minds.* London: Fontana.

Department for Education and Employment (1999) *The National Numeracy Strategy.* London: HMSO.

Frawley, P. (1992) 'Classification Programs and Databases for the Primary School', in Lodge, J. *Computer Data Handling in the Primary School.* London: David Fulton Publishers, p. 19.

Lawrence, J. (1999) *The Use of Information handling Software in the Teaching of Mathematics and Science.* Unpublished Paper. London: Brunel University.

National Council for Education (1997) *Making Sense of Information.* London: National Council for Education.

Papert, S. (1982) *Mindstorms.* Cambridge, Mass: Harvester Press.

Papert, S. (1993) *The Children's Machine.* Cambridge, Mass: Harvester Press.

Parry, E. (2000) *Programmable Robots: a Small Scale Study.* Unpublished Paper. London: Brunel University.

Straker, A. and Govier, H. (1996) *Children using Computers (Second Edition).* London: Nash Pollock, p. 36.

Trier, O. (1999) *Using ICT to Support Learning.* Unpublished Paper. London: Brunel University.

Wood, D. (1990) *How Children Think and Learn.* Oxford: Basil Blackwell, p. 183.

Websites

www.standards.dfee.gov.uk/numeracy
www.mape.org.uk
www.becta.org.uk
www.ngfl.gov.uk
www.vtc.ngfl.gov.uk
www.atm.org.uk
www.microworlds.com

CHAPTER 5

Developing problem-solving skills in mathematics

RACHEL FAIRCLOUGH

> *The ability to solve problems is at the heart of mathematics*
> (Cockcroft 1982:73)

Over 20 years ago the importance of problem solving within the teaching of mathematics was overwhelmingly apparent and often not present within the classroom practice of many teachers. The development of the role of problem solving in the mathematics classroom is substantiated by more recent applications of teaching and learning through the National Numeracy Strategy (NNS) Framework. One of the major five strands in the NNS is entitled problem solving. (DfEE 1999). The content of this chapter will include aspects of learning and teaching and their relationship to practical issues within classroom teaching of problem solving. A selection of different types of problems will be used as examples throughout. There is limited literature available from research into problem solving that focuses on the exact teaching strategies that generate improved problem solving approaches in children (Askew and Wiliam 1995). Starting with the premise that the skill or ability defined as 'problem solving' can be taught or trained at an early age; undoubtedly the careful contribution of the class teacher will show an improvement in the time taken, breadth of skills and confidence when a child is presented with a novel problem to solve. In addition, access to material on the Internet, computer games and national, even international, testing have contributed to the status of problem solving today.

In this chapter I will consider the following aspects of problem solving:

- the establishment of problem solving in the school curriculum;
- issues arising when teaching problem solving – an analysis of problem solving in practice;
- can problem solving be taught – the teacher's role when training children to solve problems effectively.

These issues will be viewed from different approaches – some well established, others based on personal observation and shared teaching experiences.

A definition of problem solving

The initial stage of defining 'problem solving' requires an understanding of what a problem is and when can a problem be considered solved. An understanding of both these aspects is essential for any teacher of mathematics to ensure that appropriate problems are presented to individual children. This chapter will examine eight different problems I have regularly used in mathematics lessons and make suggestions for teacher use, including guiding children towards an appropriate conclusion. In the Cockcroft Report, problem solving is defined as 'an ability to apply mathematics to a variety of situations' (p. 73). This definition is applicable both to the types of problems described in this chapter and the approach used to analyse them. I have considered the mathematical skills required for each problem in parallel with the skills and procedures attributed to solving any type of problem, including those not obviously mathematical in structure.

Development of problem solving

As a result of generally accepted thinking on teaching mathematics at the start of the 1980s, investigational work, not problem solving, was introduced into primary and secondary schools in this country.

The time spent on such activities varied from once a week in the most enthusiastic schools to once a year – 'because we have to!' The activities were sometimes over-contrived and even isolated from the mathematical skills a child had experienced during the same year. The early experiences of investigative work were at best well integrated and relevant to child experience in all areas of the curriculum but at worst an 'add-on' activity, part of the year's work as required when teaching from the National Curriculum.

Teachers who were taught problem-solving strategies and skills using mechanistic methods when they were children had to make a shift in their own thinking and mathematical practice. I found I had to make many changes in my teaching of investigations. The project approach, collating knowledge in an attractive presentation, was not specific enough to allow definition of the precise mathematical skills and knowledge used, nor was it flexible enough to allow experience of the range and variety of strategies or processes. Therefore a more careful scrutiny of the extent to which essential strategies and processes could be taught was necessary.

Although in recent years, an investigation is usually described as a type of problem, the terms problem and investigation have considerable overlap in interpretation.

Problem solving today

The National Curriculum Attainment Target 1, *Using and Applying Mathematics*, included investigational work as an essential part of teaching at Key Stages 1, 2, 3 and 4, throughout the compulsory years of schooling from 5 to 16 years (DfEE /QCA 1999) .

Each Programme of Study (PoS) in the National Curriculum begins with a relevant breakdown of how *Using and Applying Mathematics* should be taught. These sections are further subdivided into three parts: problem solving, communicating and reasoning. I constructed Table 5.1 by counting the number of separate teacher's guidance 'bullet' points for each of the three parts. Before reading my comments about the contents of the table make a judgment yourself on the allocation of bullet points at each key stage for each PoS.

Table 5.1 An analysis of the Using and Applying section for each Programme of Study in the National Curriculum (1999)

Programme of Study	Problem solving Communicating or Reasoning	Key Stage 1	Key Stage 2	Key Stage 3	Key Stage 4
Number &	Problem solving	4	5	5	4
Algebra	Communicating	2	4	3	5
(KS3&4 only)	Reasoning	3	2	4	4
Shape	Problem solving	3	4	3	3
Space	Communicating	1	3	4	4
Measures	Reasoning	2	1	7	6
Handling	Problem solving		5	7	7
Data	Communicating		2	3	3
	Reasoning		1	3	3

Table 5.1 indicates little change from Key Stage 3 to Key Stage 4 but the highlighted rows clearly indicate how problem solving develops across the age groups within each PoS. The three parts or strands used to define the teaching of *Using and Applying Mathematics* cannot be separated. Although the strand called problem solving is the only one referred to in this chapter, communicating and reasoning are an integral part of any solution to a problem. As an illustrative example, the numbers in the table indicating reasoning skills increase dramatically at Key Stages 3 and 4. This reflects the phase when geometrical proofs become part of the curriculum for the PoS shape, space and measures.

Can problem solving be taught?

Such explicit guidelines within the National Curriculum (see Table 5.1) and more recently the National Numeracy Strategy for teaching problem solving suggest to a teacher that problem solving can be taught in the mathematics classroom. However, my experience indicates that many problem-solving strategies develop through 'training' rather than teaching. The training situation occurs when learnt mathematical skills and latent thinking processes are applied and used in response to a particular type of problem. It is relevant at this point to examine the approaches to problem solving used by different researchers into mathematics education.

Early in the evolvement of problem solving in the mathematics classroom, Leone Burton stated that 'problem solving cannot be taught' (Burton 1986). An interesting statement within a book containing a wealth of interesting problems for children to solve, each problem requiring, according to Burton, no more skills than the child already has. An emphasis is placed on nurturing the natural curiosity of children; starting at their own level of understanding and by using questioning techniques to elicit skills, already present, to solve similar problems.

For example:

> **How many handshakes take place between twenty people if everyone shakes hand once?**

The role of the teacher in this situation may be to present the problem in such a way that the curiosity aroused in the individual child will generate a solution to the problem. If the solution is not immediately forthcoming, the strategies and application of current mathematical skills will help to focus and maintain 'Procedures' essential to the process of solving any problem.

The 'Procedures' used to solve the problems are described in the book itself. Burton suggests a three-part approach: **Entry, Attack** and finally **Review** or **Extension**. The three-part approach is further subdivided into 32 precise actions, for example 'Work backwards' is part of the **Attack** and 'Communicate' is part of the **Review–Extension**. Comparisons with the terms used in the National Curriculum document suggest that the definition of some terms have evolved in both interpretation and status. Such a detailed analysis (Burton 1986 p. 26) may make a challenging checklist of actions for both teacher and child but undoubtedly allows the 'Procedures' to be located, categorised and developed. Different strategies labelled skills are listed (Ibid. p. 27), under five different headings. For example 'Skills for Handling Information' are often referred to as 'process' skills, whereby a process can be applied to a novel problem and a solution will be the result. A process skill for handling information is 'Sorting and Ordering'.

It is the strategies, the mathematical skills or 'tools' that can be taught, which would enhance the teaching environment within which problems may be more easily solved. The timing of teaching mathematical skills may vary. The teaching can take place before the introduction of the problem or the problem can be adapted to allow learning to take place during the stages leading to the final solution. Please note that I am not referring to the process as a skill, although the processes listed later in Table 5.5 have many similarities with the skills

Table 5.2   A comparison between the approach suggested for GCSE course work investigations and the approach suggested by Burton for primary school problem solving. Italic type indicates the higher level of investigation at GCSE

Recommended GCSE textbook (Kent (ed) 1996)	Leone Burton's Skill (S) or Procedure (P)	
Make sure you understand the problem	Explore the problem	P
	Define terms and relationships	P
	Identify information	S
Check to see if you have worked on a similar problem. If you have try to make use of this experience	Try related problems	P
	Use one solution to find others	P
Try some simple and special cases	Try particular cases	P
	Focus on one aspect of the problem	P
	Test a hypothesis	S
Plan your work in an ordered way	Be systematic	P
	Sorting and ordering	S
	Choose a mode	S
	Scan all possibilities	S
Record what you are trying to do	Recording information	S
	Using a representation	S
	Many of the 'attack' procedures belong here	P
Record your observations	Develop the recording system	P
	Presenting information	S
	Recording information	S
Use appropriate diagrams and forms of communication	Translating between representations	S
	Partition the problem into cases	P
Record and tabulate any findings and results Predict what you think may happen and test it. This is called testing a conjecture.	Formulate and test hypotheses	P
	Communicate	P
	Presenting information	S
	Scan all possibilities	S
	Recognising patterns	S
	Predict from a pattern	S
	Test a result	S
Try to find and make use of any counter-examples		
Generalise, especially in symbols, if you can	Make a generalisation	P
Comment on your generalisations		
Explain and justify your generalisations		
Try to prove any generalisations		

Burton described. However, my own feeling is that the five skills stipulated by Burton: handling information, representing a problem, enumerating, finding patterns and testing are an essential part of the training process but underpin the 'Procedures' she describes. The skills she describes are strategies also. The five skills are further subdivided into 15 subcategories. Both the skills and procedures used in Burton's book are replicated in an adapted form in many texts used in schools, even the guidelines for General Certificate of Secondary Education (GCSE) coursework. I have compared the two approaches in Table 5.2.

It is apparent from the allocation of skill or procedure to each of the GCSE statements that the skills taught in primary school are essential for achieving at any level in the examinations taken nationally at 16 years of age. The procedures defined as essential to problem-solving at the primary age group are again indicated to be crucial to the problem solving process needed for later examinations.

The skills I am using when describing the eight problems in this chapter are pure mathematical skills and are an indispensable part of problem solving.

What is a problem?

The definition of a problem needs to be considered before continuing the description of methods used in the classroom. How would you define a problem?

From the studies discussing teaching and learning of problem solving in school-based mathematics, the main issue arises from establishing a mutually agreeable definition of a problem.

The literal interpretation of the word problem from the Greek is 'a thing thrown forward' usually defined as 'put forward as a question for discussion', but the 2001 version of The New Oxford Dictionary of English has specific references to the use of the word in physics and mathematics:

- 'an inquiry starting from given conditions to investigate or demonstrate a fact, result, or law' or more specifically referring to games/puzzles;
- 'an arrangement of pieces in which the solver has to achieve a specified result'.

Both definitions are applicable to the type of problem solving taking place in classrooms today, and imply a need for more than one definition of a problem. A more productive approach to understanding what constitutes a problem in the mathematics classroom might include an analysis of different types of problem. Even the skills and procedures suggested by Burton vary depending on the nature of the problem itself. Most classifications describe only four types of problem (Askew and Wiliam 1995). These four classifications will be used to define the selection of problems used in this chapter:

- **standard** problems are often called word problems and require interpretation prior to the application of mathematical operations;
- **non-standard** problems are problems that may not have an already defined procedure (see Burtons description of procedure above) for finding a solution;
- **real-world** problems require careful selection of relevant material and a 'model' to help manage the given information prior to producing a solution;
- **puzzles** are problems requiring unusual approaches to their solution.

Occasionally a problem will fall into more than one single classification.

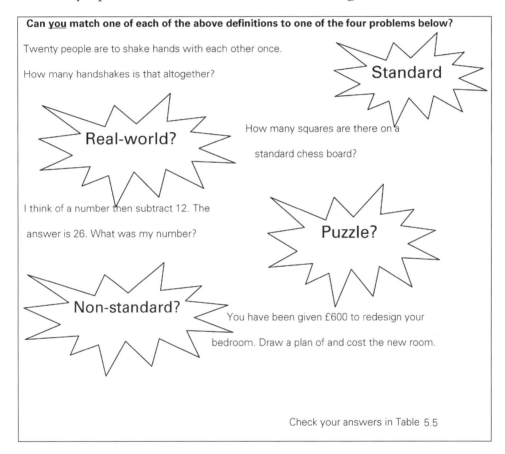

Can you match one of each of the above definitions to one of the four problems below?

Twenty people are to shake hands with each other once.

How many handshakes is that altogether?

Standard

Real-world?

How many squares are there on a

standard chess board?

I think of a number then subtract 12. The

answer is 26. What was my number?

Puzzle?

Non-standard?

You have been given £600 to redesign your

bedroom. Draw a plan of and cost the new room.

Check your answers in Table 5.5

Figure 5.1   A matching activity between four problems and the four main classifications of problem types

Askew and Wiliam (1995) found that most research has focused on standard problems in the USA while the UK research focuses on non-standard and real-life problems as part of the National Curriculum development work. A literature search would show very little established research evidence reviewing types of teaching strategies precipitating readily defined skills in problem solving, and the findings from the eight problems quoted in this chapter are from a small sample. In addition, research to date indicates little evidence linking the effects of problem-solving skill acquisition and child attainment both in mathematics and other areas of the school curriculum. Askew attributes some of these results to the type of problem: is it routine or is it realistic?

What is a realistic problem?

Routine as opposed to realistic problems at primary level provide many challenges over the teaching of problem solving (Askew 1998). Assuming the skills needed and the procedures acquired to solve problems are transferable from mathematics to other curriculum subject areas the teaching of the procedures, skill practice and the pleasure of problem solving could be effectively implemented in many primary schools even with the constraint of one numeracy lesson per day. The challenge will be how to maintain the opportunity for this transfer of learnt strategies into the secondary school years, where teachers in different curriculum areas may not communicate on a regular basis. Routine problems of the nature described by Askew are unlikely to be encountered anywhere else except in mathematics classes, although the skill and procedures may be used in a variety of circumstances.

Non-routine problems involve 'curious' problems, a mixture of non-standard and puzzles; the most stimulating are usually 'real'.

For example:

> *How many 2p pieces will be needed to make a stack as tall as you?*

The non-routine and realistic problems are the ones that encourage a child's engagement in a task, thus encouraging any potential problem solver to approach similar challenges positively.

The preceding sentences would provide convincing reasons for problem solving to be an integral part of every school curriculum, allowing each child to develop an unique repertoire of skills and procedures that may be used both inside and outside the mathematics classroom.

The 'transfer' of problem-solving strategies

I have attempted to summarise the information discussed so far and created seven 'advantages' of problem-solving training. These are listed in Table 5.3 and teachers may notice a resemblance to learning objectives. Using the list in Table 5.3 try to note any curriculum subject area, apart from mathematics, that uses the strategies listed in the first column. Part of the table has been filled in for you, but you are free to disagree.

Table 5.3   A checklist of the advantages developed through problem solving in mathematics and their relationship with other curriculum areas

Advantage of using a problem-solving approach The pupil:	Example of curriculum subject area
A. Uses arithmetic operations appropriately.	
B. Realises that a multi-solution approach may be effective and one answer may be only part of the whole solution.	
C. Considers the context of the problem not just the calculation.	
D. Incorporates estimating and approximating strategies as an integral part of the approach.	*D. Playing rounders …*
E. Regularly employs checking and re-evaluating strategies.	
F. Interprets and analyses facts and data.	
G. Uses a range of oral skills; specific vocabulary, reasoned debate and discussion prompted by both provided and discovered evidence.	*G. English, role play…*

How many did you find? Five, six? At least one of the advantages had more than one curriculum area? Many National Curriculum Programmes of Study use the advantages labeled B to G. This 'reciprocated' situation may enhance progress in mathematics and in non-mathematical subjects as transfer of those strategies; either skills or procedures may be encouraged at every relevant opportunity.

Some problems

Recent research indicates that problem-solving skills are closely related to thinking skills.

Try the next section for yourself before reading any more.

TASK 1: How many squares are there on a standard chessboard?

Allow yourself five minutes to work out the answer to the task above, mentally.

Only write the number of squares as your answer.

Table 5.4   An analysis of some different answers to the 'Chessboard problem'

Now tick the **thoughts, skills** and **procedures** you used. Select from the list below.

You wrote <u>64</u>:

- knowledge of the size of a chessboard;
- knowledge of squares, e.g. an 8 × 8 board will have 64 one-unit squares;
- counting;
- multiplication of single digit numbers;
- square numbers.

You wrote <u>92</u>:

Select any from the above list and

- visualisation of the chessboard;
- visually divide the square into different sized squares;
- select a strategy: elimination, systematically count …
- addition.

You wrote <u>204</u>:

Select any of the above thoughts and

- accepting that different squares can overlap.

You were unable to write a single number you felt confident in:

Select any of the above thoughts and

- knowledge that your mental checking procedures were not accurate;
- lacking confidence to do mental calculations without written confirmation;
- lacking confidence to do mental calculations without verbal confirmation;
- knowing the answer 64 was too simple but did not know what to do next;
- you have never attempted to solve a problem like this before.

All of the above responses are appropriate for the problem set and may be experienced by any person, including children in primary school presented with a problem. There are several answers; the 'correct' answer depends on the way the question has been interpreted. The teacher is probably essential during the presentation of a problem for generating confidence within each child and directing children towards understanding the type of problem itself. I believe some more examples of problems actually used in the mathematics classroom will help explain some of the practical aspects of trying to solve problems.

An analysis of problem solving in practice

Listed below are selected problems appropriate for children studying at Key Stages 1 and 2 and accompanying descriptions of the mathematical skills and processes involved in their solution. A detailed analysis of the problems can be found at the end of the descriptions (Table 5.5). The tables summarise the qualities of each problem.

For the following set of eight different problems, a selection of pupil responses are provided combined with a brief analysis of the type of problem and, when appropriate, possible teaching approaches.

Problem 1

Number at Key Stage 1

I think of a number, then subtract 12. The answer is 26. What was my number?

(Framework, DfEE 1999)

This is a one-step operation with only one solution.

An oral explanation may be the minimum required but a number sentence will show how this problem was solved.

Pupil responses:

'count on from 26 up to the number'

'add twelve and 26'

'four more makes 30 and the eight left makes 38'

'26 take 12 makes 14'

The fourth response requires further 'word' analysis work.

Problem 2

Number at Key Stage 2

In a dance there are three boys and two girls in every line. 42 boys take part in the dance. How many girls take part?

(Framework, DfEE 1999)

This is a multi-step operation with only one solution.

An explanation of how the problem is solved may be recorded using numbers signs and symbols.

Pupil responses:

Jon gave an oral response of *'there are 14 groups of three boys making 42 altogether. The same number of groups for the girls means two fourteens. Which makes 28. Girls, 28 girls.'*

The two examples below were written suggestions though the symbols used in the original child's work were little stick people!

$3 \times B = 42$ <u>OR</u>   BBBGG

$B \qquad = 14$ BBBGG

$2 \times 14 = 28$ girls   BBBGG

:

repeated until there are 42 B symbols.

The G symbols are totalled and the number 28 is written down.

Problem 3

Handshakes

There are 20 people in a room. Each person shakes hands once with every other person. How many handshakes will that be in total?

This problem could be called an investigation. It has one solution but the variety of methods leading to that solution may require the process of generalising.

The explanation is considered almost more important than the final single number solution, the implication being that the explanation is the solution.

This type of problem requires a realisation by the child that a repeated diagram or calculation is possible but is not the most simple or 'elegant' method. The skills and Procedures defined by Burton are applicable to this type of problem and may be used by a teacher to describe the approach and stages required by any child.

The problem is non-standard and therefore viewed by children when first introduced to it as a new problem requiring a new process for solution. The role of the teacher is crucial at the initial stage to ensure that the novelty of the problem does not become overwhelming and thus a threat to the child. The response 'can't do it' used to occur frequently in some classrooms. The teacher may reassure the children that the problem is well within their ability.

The 'handshakes' activity invites, almost begs for, a lively interactive demonstration of the problem itself at the start of the lesson. The confidence gained by every child, of all abilities, through a clear understanding of the problem itself may lead to an increased confidence in the mathematical approach to the solution.

Teachers are not in total agreement over the preparation for such an investigation, but a practical example between a few children helps. The minimum mathematical skill required apart from understanding the way numbers are written and ordered is addition. The ultimate, most 'elegant' process requires multiplication, proportion and interpretation of information in tables and diagrams, symbolisation and generalisation skills. Perhaps the most notable skill is the generalisation skill that once acquired will expand the child's repertoire of non-standard problems and hasten the problem's conclusion.

At the start of the lesson the estimate of the answer to the problem elicits interesting responses from the children ranging from:

'20'   '400'   '100'   '180'   and   'too many'   'lots'

(other responses do occur, often unpredictable with good reasoning from the child).

At this stage the teacher may consider the individual thought processes creating the different answers.

'20' – this answer may indicate a total or partial misunderstanding of the problem itself.

'400' – this answer indicates a child with a range of mathematical skills and an understanding of the problem itself confident enough to make a reasonable conjecture.

'100' – some mathematical skills shown here, child has confidence but probably using guessing skills rather than reasoning skills.

'180' – either a sophisticated 'thinker', who has mathematical skills and has thought through several stages of the problem or a good guess!

'lots' – this child may need more confidence during the early stages of solving the problem or may lack the mathematical skills to mentally consider three digit numbers.

At the next stage of the lesson introducing the problem, the thinking and application of those thought process should be considered. Alternatively, a selection of the **'Entry'** and **'Attack'** Procedures as described by Burton may be used. The problem is too complex to allow children to merely describe their process orally; it is certainly worth 'modelling' a many-stages problem using oral answers only to exemplify the need for written or diagrammatic record (for an example see Figure 5.2.) of each part of the process. A description of 'modelling' will include supporting children's own methods, not merely following another individual's procedure (Askew 1998).

The 'able' child's response

An able child may be able to provide solution with no guidance and little written evidence once the rules of the problem have been restructured into a series of hypotheses and the logical deductions have been made.

For example James's response was
'Each of 20 people must shake hands with 19 others, as they cannot shake hands with themselves. That means 19 handshakes twenty times but this will be half many because TWO people only shake hands once.'
Daniel drew two parallel lines with 20 named or numbered 'people' on each line. The lines were joined by a mass of crossed lines representing each joining of hands!
An able child will be able to explain the solution through adding the 19 starting handshakes to the next 18 then 17 then 16 down to 1 shake at the end:

$$19 + 18 + 17 + 16 + \ldots\ldots + 3 + 2 + 1.$$

However, understanding the solution does not necessarily mean that the child will easily provide the proof or checking mechanism. Prior to this stage a generalisation may be attempted using the evidence within the solution. The idea that a general rule that works for a few probably works for all parts of the evidence provided within the same problem is not new to children studying mathematics at Key Stages 1 and 2. Even at Reception level the use of comparative words such as 'smaller' and 'bigger' is important for the development of problem-solving skills where a general rule is found. The word 'more' may be considered a type of general rule itself.

The teacher may then create the cornerstone for future problem solving of the non-standard investigational type. At the next stage of problem solving an insight into the systematic approach may aid children's progress. This may be presented either as a reminder or as a taught process. The National Numeracy Strategy advocates 'estimate, calculate, check' and, when a problem is worked through, this sequence may be assumed to be taking place, although it should be noted that these three stages are not exactly equivalent to the three stages of problem solving described by Burton, '**Entry, Attack, Review/Extension**' but there are similarities.

Within the 'calculate' or '**Attack**' part of this approach to problem solving is contained the specialism that makes problem solving a unique aspect of mathematics or, as Cockcroft asserts, contains the heart of mathematics. The systematic aspect of problem solving is not essential to every problem but may enhance the rate of analysis and allows the child to develop methods for later use when more complex or mathematically demanding problems are presented. Many problems can be solved without such an approach but this is unlikely to provide a child with a strong framework for future problem solving for all types of problems.

The average child's response

Another beginning strategy may be to 'choose some simple cases'. Handshakes allows simple, small groups to be looked at and the number of handshakes counted. The written description may use diagrams or symbols but the data can be collated in a sequential format within a table.

Number of people	Number of handshakes
1	0
2	1
3	3
4	6

Generalising about rules and patterns appearing as the data is collected, testing those rules with previously collected or predicted data, possibly changing the generalisation or accepting it and ultimately using it to solve the problem – all this requires a relaxed 'playful' approach to the problem within a systematic approach.

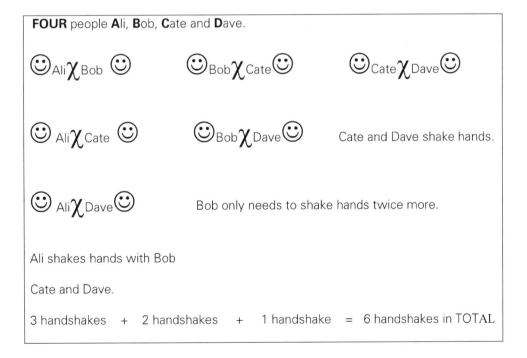

Figure 5.2   A diagrammatic explanation of the Handshakes problem between four people

The child who has chosen to draw the individuals shaking hands may choose about four or five people to start with (Figure 5.2). A child may recognise that the pattern of numbers recorded in the table is that of triangle numbers, thus recalling from memory a previously experienced pattern. This child may be able to predict the next and final solution using the knowledge of the pattern. Although this is not an essential part of primary development, the formula for h (the number of handshakes) expressed in terms of p (the number of people) is

$$h = \frac{1}{2} p (p - 1)$$

Problem 4

Lost pet

Lucy has lost her cat. The cat is the same age as Lucy and usually follows her half-way to school. When Lucy returned home after school the cat was not waiting for food in the usual place. How should Lucy try to find her pet?

This problem is again a 'real'-world problem with varied solutions and varied methods. Is this a mathematical problem? Should this type of problem be considered in the same curriculum area as numeracy? The answers to these questions are debatable and the decision to use any problem in the classroom rests with the individual preferences of the teacher.

The skills required for problem solving remain the same and many of the processes are the same. It is a problem involving time, distance, shape and space, maps, memory, visualising and an extremely systematic approach. Depending on the method decided upon to solve this problem, even collecting data and writing questionnaires will raise the solution to a high level of expertise, Year 7 in the handling data teaching programme defined within the Framework (DfEE 2001).

The problem is specific but has no one solution and the variety of solutions and their preceding methods provide avenues into other curriculum areas. The key process involved here is making assumptions. If the investigators decide the cat went home after the walk half-way to school, this is an assumption as there is no evidence for this until data have been collected through questionnaires or equivalent. The assumption keeps the problem focused on one place, home. This may prove beneficial to the teacher and allow practice in non-numerical mental skills and using correct vocabulary when memorising a route through their house.

Problem 5a

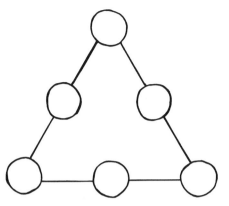

Put 1, 2 or 3 in each circle so each side adds up to five.

Figure 5.3 Arithmogon

Problem 5b

This problem is a variation on the oral and mental starter called here 'Miranda's Morning Maths' based on the television 'Countdown' programme. The children may choose any operation or combination of operations to find the answers provided. The solution in this activity is the chosen procedure as both starting point and finishing point are given.

If 2, 3, 5, 10 are the start numbers and the list of answers are 25, 50, 15, 20, 250, any correct mathematical operation(s) may be accepted using only the start numbers listed. The teacher requires the children to practise operations with multiples of 5 and 10 in this case. A type of activity allowing children to view the variety of correct but different approaches may be a valuable part of problem-solving training.

For example:

$(2 + 3) \times 5 = 25$ and $(5 \times 10) \div 2 = 25$ which is the 'correct' method?

These two types of problem have a variety of solutions, occasionally the apparently different solutions are the same, in the case of arithmogons possible rotations of each other, rather than actual numerically different solutions. The use of puzzles using a repeated 'skeleton' or 'form' is important for the apparent familiarity of the problem. Children can feel confident that they have successfully met a similar type before, thus allowing the teacher to manipulate the complexity of the task. The teacher can differentiate for ability or even skill areas; fractions or decimals as a change from whole numbers, multiplication instead of subtraction.

A repeated skeleton for the problem also allows children to try out their own problem writing talents.

Problem 6 A similar problem is used by Casey and Koshy (1995) with 7 and 8 year olds.

Redesign your bedroom (Koshy 2001)

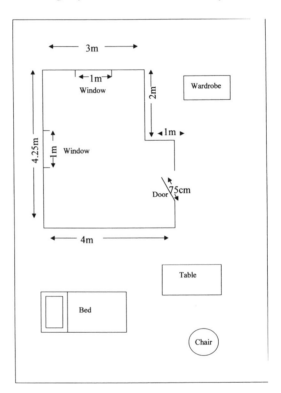

Your parents have offered to redesign your bedroom now you have grown out of the small bed used when you were young. They have given you a limit of £600 and an Argos catalogue. Choose the furniture that you need in your bedroom. A plan of your bedroom is provided. Place the furniture in the correct place in your bedroom.

Figure 5.4   A plan of your room

This is a standard or 'real' life problem with many solutions but a limited number of methods. Each child may collect, classify, sort and interpret data; money and measuring calculations are required and drawing skills for representing the solution are essential.

The approach used is systematic and testing; analysing and eliminating are parts of the main problem-solving process incorporating estimating and checking throughout the activity.

Problem 7 The software for this problem and a simpler version called Tadpoles is available through SMILE mathematics (*micro*SMILE 2001).

Frogs

What is the minimum number of moves required to change the positions of the frogs so the yellow frogs move to the lily pads occupied by the blue frogs and the blue frogs move to the lily pads occupied by the yellow frogs? There is one blank lily pad in the middle. The frogs can only move in a particular way.

Each frog can only move in one direction.
Each frog can slide into an empty space.
Each frog can jump over a frog of a different colour.

This is a puzzle and is non-standard and there is only one final numerical solution to the problem as it is phrased above. In a similar manner to the handshakes problem, the use of generalisation to prove the minimum number of moves is not necessary for finding the single solution.

Using the context of a problem

The main difference between the solution to the frogs problem and the handshakes problem is that the context of the frogs problem provides extension material and challenging problems for the most able children in the class.

The handshakes problem has a context that allows limited development, as people only have two hands and increasing numbers or introducing proportional numbers of people greeting each other is the limit of the extension, unless aliens with unusual appendages are introduced!

The frogs problem allows changes in the rules, changes in the number of frogs on each side, changes in the number of spaces, changes in the number of different colours and an extra dimension could be introduced for exceptionally ambitious children. All within the same context but each time asking 'what if …?'

The minimum number of moves for the puzzle described above is 15.

Problem 8

Chessboard

How many squares are there on a standard chessboard?

This is a puzzle that requires an understanding of the nature of the question. At face value an understanding of the size of the board and possibly the game of chess may be necessary. However, once the answer sixty-four has been suggested as incomplete, a systematic process of analysis is required. This problem, apparently simple to answer, relying on memory and specific knowledge, is an investigation of a similar type to that of the handshakes investigation. There is only one solution and, for the context defined in the question, allows little extension. Once the child realises that different sizes of squares may be considered, calculations including diagrams, tabular representation of the data and multiplication and addition skills – even some understanding of square numbers – may be used.

The single solution to the problem set is:

$$(8 \times 8) + (7 \times 7) + (6 \times 6) + (5 \times 5) + (4 \times 4) + (3 \times 3) + (2 \times 2) + (1 \times 1)$$

Diagrams will help the understanding of this question greatly, for example Figure 5.5 illustrates one type of diagram.

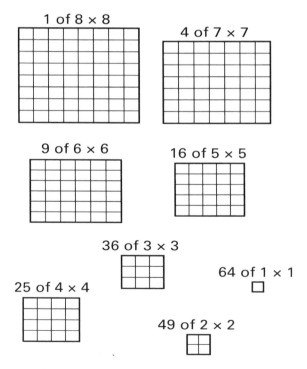

Figure 5.5   A diagram to help solve the 'Chessboard' problem

A summary of the eight problems

Table 5.5 summarises the problem, type of activity and mathematical skill used, possible processes used during the solution and the most appropriate learning objectives from the NNS Framework.

Further explanation of the words describing the process can be found at the end of the references section in the chapter.

Problem index:
1. Number at Key Stage 1
2. Number at Key Stage 2
3. Handshakes
4. Lost pet
5. Arithmogon
6. Bedroom problem for £600
7. Frogs
8. Chessboard

Throughout the short descriptions of skills and processes involved in approaching different types of problems, two aspects of the National Numeracy Strategy have not been mentioned. Firstly, I will add a section on the role of Information and Communication Technology (ICT) in problem solving, looking at two very different approaches currently practised in this country. Secondly, I will include a brief section mentioning the importance of mental skills, more details of which can be found in Chapter 3.

Information and Communications Technology (ICT)

Calculators are not advocated as essential for problem solving. The nature of the skills involved is unlikely to need support from calculators. An exception would be when the energies of the child are required for the strategy rather than the calculation.

Tony Gardiner, who has coordinated the UK Mathematical Challenges at secondary school level (ages 11–15 years) for several years insists that all the problems set in the challenges are done without a calculator. He believes that 'good problems make children think, and then learn from their mistakes' (Gardiner 1996:iv) The onus is therefore on the problem setter or the teacher to provide the appropriate problem. He also adapts the usual school textbook language, thus encouraging children to develop the skill of making mathematical sense of simple problems without the clues usually present in the 'familiar, predictable, highly suggestive language'. The techniques are standard one-step routine questions with multiple-choice answers but each problem needs to be understood, interpreted

Table 5.5   A summary of the eight problems

Problem activity	Type of activity	Mathematical skills	Process	Learning objectives from *Framework*
1. Number at Key Stage 1	Standard word problem **ONE solution** **Limited methods**	Addition, subtraction, commutative law	• classifying • undoing • testing	• solve simple word problems set in 'real life' contexts and explain how the problem was solved
2. Number at Key Stage 2	Standard word problem **ONE solution** **ONE method**	Addition, subtraction fractions, ratio, proportion	• classifying • combining • making rules • symbolising • testing	• use all four operations to solve word problems involving numbers in 'real life'
3. Handshakes	Non-standard 'word' problem **ONE solution** **Varied methods**	Visualising, kinaesthetic demonstration, addition, multiplication	• conjecturing • making rules • generalising • changing rules • symbolising • testing • proving	• organising and using data • making decisions • reasoning or generalising about numbers or shapes • identify and use appropriate operations
4. Lost pet	'Real'-world problem **Varied solutions** **Varied methods**	Memorising facts, number, distance, time. Visual representation	• guessing • systematising • hypothesising • reasoning from assumptions	• reasoning and generalising • identify and use appropriate operations involving quantities • explain methods and reasoning

Table 5.5 (cont.)

5. Arithmogon	Puzzle **Limited solutions** **Varied methods**	Four operations and their inverses. Commutative law	• classifying • testing • making rules	• choose and use appropriate number operations to solve problems
6. Bedroom problem for £600	Standard problem or 'real' life **MANY solutions** **Varied methods**	Visualisation. Addition, subtraction, area, money calculations	• making rules • changing rules • demonstrating • testing • interpreting diagrams	• reasoning or generalising about shapes • use all four operations to solve money problems
7. Frogs	Puzzle – non-standard **ONE solution** **Varied methods**	Kinaesthetic interpretation, visualisation, four operations, representative diagrams	• making rules • symbolising • hypothesising • testing • proving • generalising	• solve mathematical problems • explain and recognise patterns and relationships • use a symbol to stand for an unknown • generalise and predict • extend by asking 'What if. . . .'
8. Chessboard	Puzzle **ONE solution** **Varied methods**	Memorising facts, addition, multiplication, visualisation	• classifying • conjecturing • justifying • testing • ordering • interpreting diagrams	• recognise patterns • use an appropriate number operation and method of calculating

and quickly responded to. Some questions ask for more than one-step in their solution and a routine method will not be appropriate in many cases. The 'setting' of a problem may include an element of surprise and above all the questions are designed to be fun. The inappropriateness of calculators in a mathematics classroom is summarised by Gardiner in the statement that 'mathematics is a mental universe'. This is a view held by many mathematicians but I have found that ICT used appropriately can be an aid to mathematical concept development rather than a hindrance. The problems within the UK challenges are designed for the more able 35 per cent of the population.

At this juncture it is appropriate to mention another test for more able children, the World Class tests, a project which started in 1999. Encouragingly, since the end of 2001 this is available for any pupils but in particular those aged 9 or 13 years.

> *The problem solving in World Class tests means applying existing knowledge, skill and experience to unfamiliar situations.*   (QCA 2001)

The similarity between this statement and that read in the Cockcroft report twenty years ago is striking. In addition to the understanding of a problem, the use of a computer in the test is essential as the tests are largely computerised with few if any paper-based questions. Unlike the questions in the UK Mathematics Challenge, these tests are not multiple choice, but are timed. The problems are 'real' problems within the context of science, design and technology or mathematics. The role of ICT for these problems is to allow exploration of a wider range of tasks than is possible with just pencil and paper. The website has examples of sample questions illustrating the flexibility of this type of problem.

Role of mental arithmetic

My classroom observations reveal mental arithmetic as crucial to any problem-solving method. Without access to numerical mental skills, the problem solver may be severely hindered. Certain types of problems allow mental skills to be used but other types require mental arithmetic skills, for example an arithmogon solution may indicate other skills than problem solving if written methods or calculators are used. A comprehensive knowledge of number bonds and facts about the four operations will speed up any process during part of the solution to a problem.

So can problem solving be taught?

The National Numeracy Strategy, used in primary schools for some time and introduced in all secondary schools at KS3 in September 2001 advocates problem solving as an integral part of standard lessons; both the 'application of mathematics to every day situations within the child's experience' and the 'great deal of discussion and oral work before ... written form'. So there is an expectation that problem solving will be taught using the approaches set out in the Frameworks for the National Numeracy Strategy and the National Curriculum.

Evidence within this writing indicates that mathematical skills can be taught and the processes can be demonstrated, explained and experienced within the mathematics classroom. However, a child may not 'learn' how to solve a problem unless he or she experiences a problem, and then perceives that he or she has solved that problem effectively. Once a child has created his or her 'own' model to use when presented with another problem, the approach may be developed using taught mathematical skills and trained processes. Children with the opportunity to share approaches to problem solving with each other will be exposed to an even greater number of models and potential learning situations.

Once the child produces an oral or written response to a problem the teacher may start a record of the skills and process used by that child. The monitoring and assessment of progress resulting from the training the individual child receives in problem solving may naturally evolve from the type and frequency of problems set. Types of assessment are discussed in Chapter 8.

Summary

In this chapter I have attempted to explain some concepts of problem solving. Firstly, the establishment of problem solving as an integral part of the school curriculum, both in primary school and secondary school, was accepted and found to contain similarities across all Key Stages and many other curriculum areas of study.

Upon examination of types of problems and different words used to describe the approaches to solving problems, inconsistencies were found. Most of the inconsistencies relate to descriptions of strategies used when analysing the method of problem solving. In order to clarify these inconsistencies I suggest that **mathematical skills**, both written and mental, can be taught and applied when solving a problem. The child may have the skills available to use during the **process** of solving the problem. The process is the aspect of solving a problem that requires training; training through repetition, discussion with peers, variety of context and enjoyment of the challenge itself. ICT and mental arithmetic skills are relevant to the process and usually are used to enhance the process in some manner. The process may become faster if mental calculations occur rather than pen and paper ones, and a calculator or computer may be used to challenge the more able children and aid focus on the process instead of the calculation.

I have used eight problems of very different types to create some direction and application to the approaches to problem solving and provide easier access to some key problem-solving words and vocabulary. All eight problems have been used effectively in the classroom and may provide you with some guidance or ideas for future lessons.

Dictionary of terms used in the 'process' of problem solving

Assumption:	Something accepted as true or certain to happen without proof.
Classifying:	Arranging information in categories according to shared qualities or characteristics.
Combining:	Joining of different qualities in such a way that their individual distinctiveness is retained.
Conjecturing:	Conclusion formed on the basis of incomplete information.
Changing rules:	Altering one or more starting principles.
Demonstrating:	Clearly showing the existence or truth by giving evidence.
Generalising:	Making general or broad statements.
Guessing:	Estimating without sufficient information of being correct.
Hypothesising:	Putting something forward as a hypothesis.
Hypothesis:	A supposition or proposed explanation made on the basis of limited evidence as a starting point for further investigation.
Interpret diagrams:	Explain the meaning of, or evidence shown by, a drawing, graph, table or statistical representation.
Making rules:	Creating the principles or guidelines for an activity or strategy.
Ordering:	Arranging things in relation to each other according to a particular sequence, pattern or method.
Proving:	Testing the accuracy of a mathematical calculation through demonstrating using evidence or argument.
Reasoning from assumptions:	Find an answer to a problem using assumptions.
Symbolising:	Using symbols to represent or stand for something else.
System:	An organised scheme or method, using a set of rules.
Systematising:	Arranging according to an organised system.

Testing: Taking measures to check the quality or reliability of
                      something.
Undoing: Reversing the effects/results of a previous calculation or
                      measure.

References

Askew, M. (1998) *Teaching Primary Mathematics.* London: Hodder and Stoughton.
Askew, M. and Wiliam, D. (1995) *Recent Research in mathematics education 5–16.* London: Ofsted.
Burton, L. (1986) *Thinking Things Through.* Oxford: Blackwell.
Casey, R. and Koshy, V. (1995) *Bright Challenges.* London: Brunel University.
Cockcroft, W. H. (1982) *Mathematics Counts. Report of the Committee of inquiry into the teaching of mathematics in schools.* London: HMSO.
DfEE (1999) *The Framework for Teaching Mathematics from Reception to Year 6.* London: Department for Education and Employment.
DfEE (2001) *The Framework for Teaching Mathematics: Years 7, 8 and 9.* London: Department for Education and Employment.
DfEE and QCA (1999) *The National Curriculum for England.* London: Department for Education and Employment & Qualifications and Curriculum Authority.
Gardiner, A. (1996) *Mathematical Challenges.* Cambridge: University Press.
Kent, D. (ed.) (1996) *London GCSE Mathematics.* Oxford: Heinemann.
Koshy, V. (2001) *Teaching Mathematics to Able Children.* London: David Fulton Publishers.
Pearsall, J. (ed.) (2001) *The New Oxford Dictionary of English.* Oxford: University Press.
SMILE (2001) *MicroSMILE Mathematical Puzzles.* London: SMILE Mathematics.

Websites

www.qca.org.uk/ca/tests/wct/about_the_tests.asp
www.smilemathematics.co.uk

CHAPTER 6

Numeracy and low attaining children

JEAN MURRAY

Introduction

Concern about low attainers is currently high on the national mathematical agenda, as part of the raising standards debate. Current national initiatives addressing the needs of low attainers include numeracy booster classes for Year 6 children. These are designed for those children who need intensive, targeted support to reach Level 4 in the Key Stage 2 Standard Assessment Tasks (SATs), taken at the age of 11.

Springboard 3 and Springboard 4 are initiatives designed for children in Years 3 and 4 who have achieved Level 2C in the Key Stage 1 SATs, taken in Year 2 at the age of seven. The National Numeracy Strategy (NNS) website (2001) states that the aims of these initiatives are:

- to support the identified children and to remedy particular weaknesses in number so that they are in a better position to access and benefit from the teaching programmes (in that year of schooling) and beyond;
- to set the expectation that these children catch up with their peers;
- to help teachers prepare a teaching programme enabling children to benefit fully from the main teaching programme (for that year of schooling).

A similar programme, Springboard 5, is designed to support children in Year 5, who without intervention, would be likely to achieve Level 3 in mathematics at the end of Key Stage 2 (that is, below the national 'average' for the age group). Like the Year 6 booster classes, Springboard 5 aims to help such children achieve Level 4 in the Key Stage 2 SATs.

The aims of these initiatives reflect the national concern with raising children's mathematical achievement, particularly in relation to the Key Stage 2 SATs. Worthy and well intentioned as such initiatives may be, support for low attainers should not just be short term to facilitate passing a test; nor should it just be about raising attainment in relation to the peer group for the sake of class, school or national targets. Rather support should be about creating the foundations for long-term, on-going patterns of attainment in mathematics for each individual child.

This chapter reports on a research study into the knowledge and understanding of addition, as used in mental calculations, of a group of mathematically low attaining children. The findings show that the seven and eight year olds in the sample group could be divided into three groups according to the calculation methods they used. The chapter is structured as follows: the key characteristics of each group are briefly described; case studies of individual children then illustrate these characteristics. Each case study is followed by details of the teaching strategies used to enhance the children's numeracy. Finally, issues arising from the research for unlocking low attaining children's numeracy are identified and discussed.

The learning components of mathematics can be considered as facts, skills, concepts (and conceptual structures), strategies and attitudes (DES 1985; Ernest 1999). This chapter argues that in order to achieve long-term patterns of success in the subject, it is crucial that children's *confidence* and *competence* in numeracy are both raised. In other words children need both the knowledge and understanding of the relevant facts, skills, concepts and strategies (*competence* is used here as a convenient, if somewhat limited, shorthand term for this complex network of mathematical learning), and the *confidence* in their own ability to use and apply these things successfully.

Definition of mathematical low attainers

The definition of low attainers used in this chapter draws on that of Haylock (1991). He rejects a variety of labels for children who struggle with mathematics, including 'less able children', 'slow learners' and 'underachievers', because of their connotations of negativity. He opts for the term 'low attainers' to describe children 'who need special help and provision in mathematics' and whose progress in the subject is a cause for concern (p. 10). These are the children who would be in the bottom 25 per cent of 'a notional ability range for their peer group' (p. 10). The reasons for such patterns of low attainment in mathematics are 'varied, complex, idiosyncratic and unpredictable' (p. 9).

Such a definition inevitably involves some norm-referenced judgements in that low attaining children are 'assessed' in relation to their more able peers. But this should not obscure the all important fact that the majority of these children are also underachieving in relation to *their own potential in mathematics*. And the key focus in 'unlocking' numeracy for low attaining children is that such work should further the development of this *individual potential*.

Low attaining children and mental mathematics: the research study

The study focused on 30 children at the beginning of Year 3 of their primary schooling. It looked mainly at the mental calculation methods the children used in addition, although this focus also involved a consideration of their knowledge and understanding of the operation of addition and some aspects of two-digit place value. All the children came from a large primary school in a socially and economically deprived, and ethnically diverse area of Outer London. The school closely followed the curriculum and pedagogical guidance disseminated nationwide by the NNS. At the time of the research the Year 3 children had had two years of teaching following this guidance. Their numeracy work had therefore included a heavy emphasis on mental mathematics.

The sample group was chosen in consultation with the school's mathematics coordinator and the Year 3 class teachers, using Haylock's definition of low attainers as a guide to ensure selection of an appropriate sample. The children's age varied from 8.2 years to 7.2 years, with a mean age of 7.9 at the time of the study.

Each child was assessed using a basic assessment schedule devised to find out:

- what addition facts did s/he know by heart (as instant recall knowledge)?
- what addition calculations could s/he work out or deduce? ('quick' recall)?
- what strategies did s/he use for the 'quick' recall calculations?

The emphasis was on mental mathematics throughout, although in order to ensure continuity with the NNS guidance (DfEE 1999a), the children were allowed to use written jottings to assist with the mental calculations, as and when needed. The use of fingers as counting aids was allowed, but the children had no access to other physical resources such as Multi-link or ready-made number lines. These 'rules' were clearly explained to the children prior to the assessments. The assessment schedule was focused around the following addition facts and strategies, which the NNS identifies as key objectives for the end of Year 2:

- knowledge of addition facts for all numbers to at least 10 (*for example, 6+4 as an addition bond for 10*);
- all pairs of numbers with a total of 20, doubles of all numbers to 10 and the corresponding halves;
- the use of a range of mental strategies for addition calculations, including counting on in ones or tens, partitioning, doubling, using near doubles, and putting the larger number first.

The Year 2 objective of

> count, read, write and order whole numbers to at least 100; know what each
> digit represents (using 0 as a place holder)

was also partially assessed, where appropriate, in order to analyse how the children's knowledge and understanding of two-digit place value might support their
calculation methods.

All the children were assessed using this schedule. After the analysis of the
resulting data, a representative sub-sample of nine case study children was selected
for follow-up research. This included analysis of their mathematical records back
to the Reception class and interviews with their mathematics teachers in both
Years 2 and 3 about their patterns of mathematical attainment. Based on the
findings of the study and on available curriculum guidance (see, for example,
Haylock 1991; Edwards 1998; Gross 1996), strategies for enhancing the children's confidence and competence in their mental calculation of addition were
then identified and implemented.

Analysis of the findings showed that the children could be split into three
groups, according to their calculation methods. These groups were named *continuing counters, fact clingers* and *beginning strategists.* Fifteen of the children were
defined as continuing counters, four as fact clingers, and eleven as beginning
strategists.

In the following sections of this chapter, the key characteristics of each group
are briefly described. Case studies of individual children then extend and exemplify these characteristics. Each case study is followed by details of the teaching
strategies used to enhance the children's numeracy. In order to develop both competence and confidence, the teacher strategies were tailored individually for each
child. But all of these strategies had the over-arching aims of:

- developing the children's knowledge and understanding of numeracy (their
  competence);
- enhancing confidence, particularly an 'If-I-try-I-can-do-it' attitude to mathematics work.

Continuing counters

Children in this group tackled all the sums by counting on one by one. Some
children just counted orally, either out loud or in subdued mutterings; others
accompanied their oral counting with finger counting, nods of the head or attempts to trace lines on the desktop as they counted. These movements were
obvious attempts to keep track of the oral counting. Only one child in this group
used any kind of written jotting to support his calculation. In calculating 2+8,
for example, he asked if he could draw a number line. When told that this was
fine, he proceeded to draw an intricate number line showing all the numbers

from 1–20. He then used this line to count slowly from 1 to 2 and then on for another 8 numbers until he reached 10.

The strategy of counting on in ones by low attaining children has been noted by a number of other writers (see, for example, Denvir 1984; Askew and Wiliam 1995; Barrington *et al.* 1999). Counting in this way appears to provide a kind of 'mathematical security blanket' for children who, for a variety of reasons, have not acquired a wider range of knowledge and strategies. Counting one by one may offer a sound way of calculating with small numbers, but the method has obvious disadvantages in calculations with larger numbers where errors become more likely. Over-reliance on this method may mask children's difficulties in remembering number facts, another factor which is associated with low attainers (Merttens 1997). Anghileri and Johnson (1992) argue that over-dependence on one to one counting removes the need to learn addition bonds which in turn limits the development of children's strategic methods.

The guidance issued on teaching number by SCAA (1997) identifies that children's growth in understanding of number is marked by a fundamental underlying change in what is considered as a 'unit'. In the early years of numeracy a 'unit' is a 'single whole entity' (p. 5), so counting a group of objects involves seeing each as a separate object. But as understanding grows, children progress on to understanding a 'unit' as also referring to a group of objects (*a composite unit*). This idea of the composite unit is fundamental to children's understanding of place value; once acquired, it can also be used in addition calculations, as the basis of various 'short-cut' strategies. So in addding 10+8, children can eventually progress to treating the '10' as a unit to add to a second unit of '8' (p. 6). Continuing counters in this research appeared to have either not acquired or not implemented this understanding of the composite unit in their calculation methods.

Case study 1: Carlos

In the research study Carlos counted to obtain the answer to all the sums, tackling each sum just as it was presented to him. He used his fingers to support his oral counting, so 3+6, for example, involved counting three fingers and then six more. Asked to calculate with numbers more than ten, he used all available fingers, supplemented by nods of the head. With calculations totalling ten or less Carlos achieved accurate answers; with larger numbers, not surprisingly, he frequently mis-counted. Carlos appeared to have no factual knowledge of addition bonds, and no mental calculation strategies beyond counting one by one. His knowledge of two-digit place value was generally insecure, particularly his knowledge of how to partition numbers into ones and tens.

Carlos' school records showed that he had missed a great deal of schooling in his Reception year. He had been very slow to learn to count a group of objects, experiencing difficulties particularly with organising his counting and understanding the idea of the conservation of number. But it seemed that, once Carlos had learnt to count, he had applied the idea of counting on to all addition calculations. Consequently, he focused on each number to be added as a series of single units rather than realising that it could be added as a composite unit. Success in achieving the right answer with some calculations involving small numbers encouraged Carlos to continue using his basic counting method, when he really needed to move on to develop his factual knowledge and a wider range of strategies.

Although Carlos was low attaining in number work, his teacher said that he often achieved well in space and shape work. She felt that Carlos had good spatial ability, and was a strongly 'visual learner'.

Ways forward for Carlos

The specific aim for working with Carlos was to generate and consolidate factual knowledge, underpinned by sound conceptual knowledge of addition. The strategies for achieving this aim were as follows:

- *Providing strong visual/spatial images of number facts alongside written representations of the sums.* This strategy was devised to draw on Carlos' spatial ability, and to provide him with an immediate boost to his confidence. An old set of Colour Factor rods was located at the back of the school's mathematics stock cupboard, and cannibalised by writing the numerical value on each rod. The teacher then used the rods, alongside the relevant sums, to illustrate the pattern of the basic addition bonds to ten for Carlos. The advantage of using the Colour Factor rods for this exercise, rather than Multi-link or similar individual cubes, was that the rods represented each number as a composite unit (so, for example, the 6 block was a length of wood equivalent to six single units, but the block was not marked as individual units and so could not be counted one by one). This encouraged Carlos to identify each number as a composite unit rather than as a collection of single units. After some initial work with the rods, Carlos' strong spatial sense enabled him to play a 'guess the missing number game' with the rods (see Figure 6.1).
- *Setting achievable targets.* Carlos' work with the rods was linked to targets for him to memorise and use key number facts. Carlos' parents were involved in these targets. They continued using the rods with him at home, gradually moving from playing the guessing game with the rods to playing it with flash cards with sums written on them.
- Support at home and school thus gave Carlos *opportunities to practise and use his developing knowledge.* Developing his knowledge of number patterns and relationships was important here, so that his factual knowledge was connected to his growing conceptual understanding of the operation of addition.

Using the rods again, the teacher illustrated to Carlos the commutativity of addition and the ways in which addition was the inverse of subtraction. A simple computer program 'Function Machine' helped Carlos to understand this inverse relationship further.

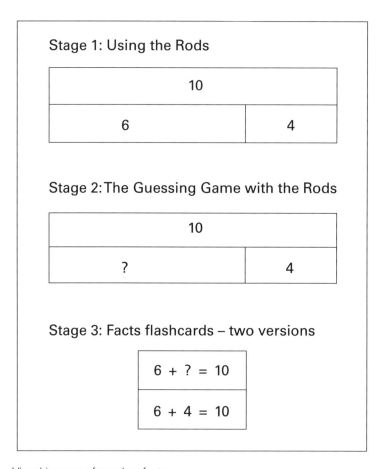

Figure 6.1   Visual images of number facts

Fact clingers

As the name of this group suggests, these children had instant recall knowledge of some addition bonds, particularly those to ten. Some of them also knew bonds involving the addition of small numbers (for example, 13+1 or 2). Using this knowledge gave the children a way of answering some of the questions on the assessment schedule quickly and easily; with most of the other questions, however, they floundered, usually resorting to guessing wildly or to counting on one by one.

These children clung to their factual knowledge, using it whenever they could.

It gave them a bank of valuable mathematical knowledge, but when they forgot these facts, problems occurred. The research showed that these facts had been learnt by rote, and the children had no underlying understanding of their *meaning*. When they forgot the facts, they therefore had no *mathematical safety net* which would enable them to re-build that knowledge. An earlier research study on able children's mental calculation strategies (see Murray 1999:164) showed how a numerate child who forgot a fact was able to go on to calculate the answer using an effective strategy, because he had a good underlying understanding of the number concepts involved. In contrast to this able child, fact clingers seemed to have no back up strategies beyond one by one counting.

This also meant that they had no *mathematical springboard* from which to generate new knowledge. The 1999 study (Murray p. 165) showed how another able child, with the support of careful teacher questioning, was able to use her existing knowledge of number facts, alongside her conceptual understanding, as a springboard to create new knowledge. There were no indications in this research study that fact clingers could forge new knowledge in this way. Their factual knowledge therefore had limited value.

Case study 2: Amy

Amy's records showed a pattern of underachievement at mathematics going back to Year 1. They also showed that she had often been very anxious about her work, particularly about 'getting sums wrong'. Not surprisingly, this anxiety had intensified at the time of her SATs in Year 2. Amy's parents had tried to ease her anxiety by helping her to learn number facts at home. They had set up a careful programme of rote learning in which Amy was rewarded for memorising addition bonds.

This knowledge provided her with a valuable confidence boost, a quick fix 'solution' for her mathematical problems and anxieties. By clinging on to her knowledge of these facts she could answer – and quickly – some of the questions her teacher asked in the introduction to each Numeracy Hour lesson. But, because Amy had no understanding of the underlying mathematical concepts, her knowledge remained limited. Furthermore, her ongoing lack of strategies for mental calculations meant that she was restricted in her development of new knowledge.

In the research study Amy answered half of the sums involving addition bonds totalling ten very quickly and confidently. Attempting to answer the remaining sums of a similar size, she froze, and after long pauses, said she couldn't do the sums because she had 'forgotten' the answer. Her knowledge of number bonds to ten was therefore patchy, and her ability to calculate totals above ten was limited. Her knowledge and understanding of two-digit place value was also limited; she could count orally from 1 to 100, but when questioned had little sense of number order for numbers between 21 and 100. Partitioning two-digit numbers into tens and ones was also difficult for her. The assessment had to be finished early because Amy was becoming increasingly flustered by her inability to 'remember the answers'.

Ways forward for Amy

The specific aim was for Amy to understand the *mathematical meaning* of the number facts she was trying to memorise so diligently. The strategies for achieving this aim were as follows:

- *Working with Amy to identify a variety of visual and oral representations of addition facts.* For example, Amy was first asked to find different ways of picturing 4+6. Supported initially by her teacher, she was able to draw the sum on a number line and collect sets of four and six items to combine together. This provided Amy with explicit models of addition as both *aggregation* (Haylock (2000:208) defines this as 'two or more quantities combined into a single quantity') and *augmentation* (Haylock defines this as where 'a quantity is increased by an amount and the operation of addition is required in order to find the … increased value'). On another occasion she was asked to 'read' 4+6 in a variety of different ways, using mathematical language such as 'add', 'plus', and 'more than'.
- *Involving parents.* The class teacher set up a meeting with Amy's parents to outline and discuss the situation. Following this meeting, it was agreed that her parents would continue to give Amy regular practice of the facts that she knew, alongside developing and supporting the teacher's other strategies.
- *Experimenting with number patterns.* Amy was asked to explore different number patterns, drawing on and extending her existing knowledge. One day she took home the start of the number pattern

  10+1=
  11+1=
  12+1=

  She was asked to complete and extend the pattern to 25 and to come back to school able to discuss how and why the pattern worked. Another pattern task involved finding as many different ways as possible of solving the puzzle ? + ? = 15 and discussing any patterns she saw. Later pattern work included an emphasis on subtraction as the inverse of addition. This work was valuable in developing Amy's understanding of number relationships. It also provided creative and enjoyable ways in which Amy could use, apply and extend her existing knowledge. Amy and her parents extended this work at home using a calculator to enable the exploration of addition patterns with large numbers.

- *strengthening knowledge of two digit place value.* For Amy this involved a particular focus on developing her knowledge of the order of the numbers between 11 and 99.
- *achievable targets* for Amy were set in all of these areas, and monitored by Amy herself, her parents and the class teacher.

Beginning strategists

This group showed evidence of a range of developing strategies, used alongside some factual knowledge. Typically, beginning strategists had variable factual or instant recall knowledge of addition bonds to ten, and some knowledge of addition bonds to 20. Favoured strategies were doubling and use of near doubles, and counting on from the largest number. Some of the children could count on in tens to 100, and partition numbers up to 50, but their knowledge of two-digit place value was often not secure enough to enable them to use strategies, such as partitioning, consistently and confidently.

When figuring out the sums, beginning strategists tended to stick to just one strategy whatever the sum asked. They showed little awareness of choosing the most effective and economical method for each sum. The guidance issued by SCAA (1997) on the teaching and learning of mental mathematics identifies that some children rely on a basic range of calculating methods and 'do not look for alternative methods' or take account of number properties that 'may be obvious to the more skilled mental calculator' (p. 14).

Case study 3: Ravinder

Ravinder spoke English as an Additional Language (EAL). In the assessments Ravinder showed considerable strengths in her knowledge and understanding of mental calculation. She knew some addition bonds to ten as instant recall knowledge. She had instant recall knowledge of the 'double facts' to ten, with the exception of $4+4=8$, and some 'double facts' to 20, including $10+10$ and $8+8$. She could also use this knowledge to work out accurately other answers using a 'near-doubles' strategy (see Figure 6.2). But these were the only mental calculation strategies she used during the assessments.

Interviewer: What's 7 + 8? Can you work that out?

Ravinder: (after long pause) 15

Interviewer: Well done. How did you work that out?

Ravinder: (after some prompting) I said 7 and 7 14. 1 more 15.

Figure 6.2   Using the 'near-doubles' strategy

Ravinder's mathematics records showed a pattern of underachievement in numeracy dating back to the Reception class, linked to her struggles to make sense of mathematical language. She had had ongoing problems with understanding aspects of two-digit place value in Year 2, particularly partitioning and the names and order of numbers between 11 and 100. But her Year 2 records also showed some rapid progress in ability to solve spatial problems and puzzles requiring logical and systematic thinking.

When interviewed, Ravinder's teacher expressed considerable surprise at the extent of her instant recall knowledge and her use of the 'near-doubling' strategy. In mental mathematics sessions the teacher observed that Ravinder rarely offered an answer, and sometimes found it difficult to keep up with the pace of the lesson. Many of these sessions included discussion of the variety of methods used for calculation, including children's explanations of their methods. But Ravinder's teacher was unsure how much benefit she obtained from such discussions. Both interviewer and teacher felt that, with some additional help, Ravinder could build on her existing strengths in numeracy to become an efficient mental calculator.

Ways forward for Ravinder

The specific aims for working with Ravinder were to extend her knowledge of the different methods for mental calculation, and to consolidate and extend her conceptual knowledge and understanding of addition. The teaching and learning strategies for achieving this aim were as follows:

- *Working with a more able peer explaining and discussing mental methods.* The teacher set up daily five minute discussion sessions for Ravinder and a friend who was confident in using a wide range of mental strategies. The pair were given a small list of calculations, asked to work out the sums and then explain their calculation to one another. These sessions had two aims: firstly, they aimed to provide Ravinder with unpressurised opportunities to listen to a range of methods; secondly, they aimed to give her regular practice in explaining her own methods to develop her use of mathematical language. At regular intervals the teacher also joined in with these sessions to provide visual images of the strategies being described. For example, she drew representations of the partitioning of two-digit numbers and of calculations using an empty number line.
- *Setting achievable targets.* This strategy was used to help Ravinder to develop a wider range of factual knowledge, including knowledge of key addition bonds to 10 and then 20. After a meeting with the teacher, Ravinder's parents were involved in these targets. Each week she was set a small number of facts to practise at home. Later she also took home more complex sums and was asked to work with her parents and older siblings to find ways of using her developing factual knowledge to find the answers.

- *Developing knowledge of place value.* This work with Ravinder focused on developing her knowledge of three aspects of two-digit place value: number names, number order and partitioning. Her teacher provided additional oral practice of the number names between 10 and 100, linking this practice to the ways in which the numbers were written. The computer program 'Counter' enabled the teacher to devise a variety of ways of counting with the numbers on the computer screen. A calculator programmed with the constant function to keep adding one provided a simpler version of the same idea. Linking this counting practice to a number line enabled Ravinder to develop her understanding of number order. She also worked at partitioning two-digit numbers into tens and units. This work included use of a variety of visual, tactile and symbolic resources, including the computer game 'Highs and Lows' which provided an effective and motivating learning context.

Issues raised by the study

This was a small-scale research study, and consequently it is not possible to make generalisations from it to all low attainers. It should, however, be noted that some of the patterns found here in low attaining children's numeracy have also been identified in other studies (see, for example, Denvir 1984; Houssart 2001). The study also raises a long list of issues abut low attaining children's numeracy. From this list I have selected three main issues which teachers who struggle to support such children may well benefit from considering. These issues are as follows: the need for early diagnostic assessment of low attainers and for follow-up teaching programmes in key areas of numeracy; the use of multi-sensory teaching approaches which connect different mathematical ideas and the ways in which they are represented; and the setting of attainable targets which are understood by children, their teachers and their parents or carers.

Early diagnostic assessment of low attainers and focused teaching programmes

Young as they were, all of the case study children had a history of finding mathematics difficult, dating back to the early years of their schooling. For many years there has been an understandable reluctance to 'label' children as struggling with mathematics in these early years. But some recent initiatives in mathematics education (see, for example, Wright *et al.* 2000) indicate that this well meaning stance may lead to accumulating difficulties for the children concerned. In this study a number of the children, like Carlos, had 'trailed' difficulties with learning to count from the Reception class into Key Stage 1. Learning to count is a complex process for young children. It is also one of the foundation stones of mathematical learning. If children do not learn to count accurately and confidently at an early stage in their schooling, then their later mathematical development will inevitably be delayed. Other children in the study had, like Ravinder, struggled with early mathematical language. Acquiring, understanding and applying mathematical language is an integral part of unlocking numeracy. Many children, not just those with EAL, require additional help in understanding the complexities of this language.

All of the low attaining children in this study showed limited knowledge and understanding of two-digit place value. The variable rates at which children acquire knowledge of place value are well documented in studies reaching back to the Cockcroft Report (1982). This body of research shows that some children 'trail' difficulties in understanding place value from Key Stage 1 well into Key Stage 2, and on into their secondary schooling. Yet this understanding is fundamental to developing a 'feel for number'; consequently, without this fundamental understanding of how our number system works low attainers have very limited opportunities to unlock the world of numeracy.

The National Numeracy Strategy guidance places considerable emphasis on the importance of teaching and learning in these three key areas of learning to count, place value, and developing age-range appropriate knowledge of mathematical language. But the findings of this research point to the need for additional diagnostic assessment and, where necessary, additional well-focused, teaching programmes in these three key areas for low attaining children. Appropriate and well focused early intervention in helping low attainers to count, to understand mathematical language, and to understand the concept of place value may well prevent more complex patterns of underachievement developing in later schooling.

The use of multi-sensory teaching approaches

Research conducted on behalf of the Teacher Training Agency to identify the characteristics of effective teachers of mathematics (see Askew *et al.* 1997) showed that such teachers 'connected different areas of mathematics and different ideas in the same area of mathematics using a variety of words, symbols and diagrams' (p. 2). Drawing in part on such research findings, teaching approaches which explicitly connect different mathematical ideas and the ways in which they are represented are widely advocated in current guidance on teaching mathematics. The curriculum guidance given by the NNS (DfEE 1999a), for example, suggests that there are five strategies which teachers can use to help children memorise facts: visual, oral, kinaesthetic, written recording and use of mathematical patterns. The guidance also advocates using a variety of appropriate resources to support the development of numeracy.

Such *multi-sensory teaching approaches* are important to enable all children to learn mathematics, but they are of particular importance for low attainers. The low attainment of the children in this study derived in part from their mono-dimensional *understanding* of how to tackle addition problems. For Carlos counting on one by one had become his only method of addition; for Amy addition bonds that she struggled to recall served the same function. Ravinder, despite her obvious potential in mathematics, re-cycled the same basic methods of calculation. The potentially stimulating, rich and inter-connected world of early numeracy had become restricted and fragmented for them. Multi-sensory teaching approaches to mathematics enable connections within and across that world to be made in meaningful ways. The use of the blocks to give Carlos visual images and tactile experiences of the addition facts to ten gives an example of this approach.

Creating achievable targets and learning partnerships

The pedagogical and curriculum guidance given by the NNS (DfEE 1999a) and currently being implemented in a large number of English primary schools identifies the need for teachers and children to work to key learning objectives. Target setting for groups and individuals becomes part of this process. The principle of re-visiting aspects of the numeracy curriculum at regular intervals is also implied by the schemes of work included in the Professional Development folders given to all schools. These structures are basically sound, but the pace of the curriculum and the normalised sequence of progression implied may need some adaptation for low attaining children. Teaching for low attainers needs to build (or in some cases re-build) mathematical knowledge, understanding and confidence, not to pile further incomprehensible ideas on to already shaky foundations.

It is important that low attaining children are set achievable and realistic targets that are clearly related to the outcomes of diagnostic assessments and to follow-up teaching programmes. As outlined above, there are key areas of early numeracy that need to be addressed in such programmes. But a number of children who are judged to be low attaining in their numeracy work have strengths in other areas of mathematics work. In this study, Carlos, for example, had strengths in space and shape work, and Ravinder showed strengths in problem solving. It is important that such strengths are recognised and used in target setting, since they offer important starting points for developing children's confidence in their mathematics work.

Low attaining children derive considerable benefits if their parents are involved in and well informed about their mathematical learning. Some parents may lack confidence in mathematics themselves; others may be uncertain of how they should be supporting their children. Either of these factors may cause gaps, or even contradictions, to occur between the mathematics children are learning at school and at home, as in the case of Amy's well meaning parents.

National Numeracy Strategy guidance on parental involvement in mathematics (DfEE 1999b) identifies that schools need to develop close relationships with parents, ensuring that they understand how mathematics is taught in schools and how they can help their children. They also need to understand the importance that the NNS places on mental mathematics between the ages of five and nine years, and the general importance of mathematical discussion in learning. Involving parents in achieving and setting the learning targets for low attainers is an important part of this process of partnership.

Conclusion

This chapter has drawn on the findings of a small-scale research study to identify three patterns in low attaining children's mental calculations. It has then identified a range of teaching strategies that were used to enhance the numeracy of the three case study children. Early intervention in children's numeracy to support key aspects of learning, the use of multi-sensory teaching methods, and creating achievable targets and learning partnerships have been identified as important issues in the teaching of low attainers.

The chapter has used a definition of low attainers based partly on norm referenced judgements, but it has also asserted that, more importantly, the majority of these children are underattaining in relation to *their own potential in mathematics*. The current national focus is on raising the levels of attainment of these children in relation to their more average attaining peers. Important as this issue may be on the educational agenda, we should not lose sight of the importance of simultaneously developing children's *individual potential*. The chapter shows that the key to unlocking numeracy for mathematical low attainers is to focus on enhancing this potential by using teacher strategies which develop competence and confidence in personal attainment. In this way the foundations for long-term, ongoing, individual patterns of attainment can be built.

References

Anghileri, J. and Johnson, D. (1992) 'Arithmetic operations on whole numbers: multiplication and division', in Post, T. (ed) *Teaching mathenmatics in grades K–8*. Boston, MA: Allyn and Bacon.

Askew, M., Brown, M., Rhodes, V., Wiliam, D. and Johnson, D. (1997) *Effective Teachers of Numeracy: Report of a study carried out for the Teacher Training Agency*. London: King's College, University of London.

Askew, M. and Wiliam, D (1995) *Recent Research in Mathematics Education 5–16*. London: Ofsted.

Barrington, R., Hamilton, C. and Harries, T. (1999) 'Numeracy and Low Attainers in Mathematics', *Topic* **22** Autumn.

Cockcroft, W. H. (1982) *Mathematics Counts: Report of the Committee of Inquiry into the Teaching of Mathematics*. London: HMSO.

Denvir, B. (1984) *The Development of Number Concepts in Low Attainers in Mathematics aged seven to nine years*. Kings College, London (unpublished PhD thesis).

Department of Education and Science (1985) *Mathematics from 5 to 16*. London: HMSO.

Department for Education and Employment (DfEE) (1999a) *The National Numeracy Strategy: Framework for Teaching Mathematics from Reception to Year 6*. London: DfEE.

Department for Education and Employment (DfEE) (1999b) *At Home with Numeracy*. London: DfEE.

Edwards, S. (1998) *Managing Effective Teaching of Mathematics 3–8*. London: Paul Chapman Publishing.

Ernest, P. (1999) 'Teaching and Learning mathematics', in Koshy, V., Ernest, P. and Casey, R. (eds) *Mathematics for Primary Teachers*. London: Routledge.

Gross, J. (1996) *Special Educational Needs in the Primary School*. Buckingham: Open University Press.

Haylock, D. (1991) *Teaching Mathematics to Low Attainers 8–12*. London: Paul Chapman Publishing.

Haylock, D. (2000) *Mathematics Explained for Primary Teachers*. London: Paul Chapman Publishing.

Houssart, J. (2001) 'Counting Difficulties at Key Stage Two', *Support for Learning* **16**(1).

Merttens, R. (1997) *Teaching Numeracy, Maths in the Primary Classroom*. London: Scholastic.

Murray, J. (1999) 'Mental mathematics', in Koshy, V., Ernest, P. and Casey, R. (eds) *Mathematics for Primary Teachers*. London: Routledge.

SCAA (1997) *The Teaching and Assessment of Number at Key Stages 1–3*. Discussion paper No.10. London: SCAA.

Wright, R., Martland, J. and Stafford, A. (2000) *Early Numeracy: Assessment for Teaching and Intervention*. London: Paul Chapman Publishing.

Website

www.standards.dfee.gov.uk/numeracy

CHAPTER 7

A framework for teaching mathematically promising pupils

RON CASEY

Introduction

The production and use of a framework for teaching mathematically promising pupils requires justification, explanation and evaluation. The justification will be given by referring to aspects of national policy, with appropriately selected signposts towards the need for the production of a framework. The explanation will involve an attempt to integrate personal insights, references to some authoritative sources, and experiences with the realities of teaching mathematics in schools. The evaluation of the framework requires the intrinsic merits to be acceptable to teachers so that they feel sufficiently confident to adopt it in their teaching of mathematically promising pupils. The mechanism of school-based evaluation is not being fully considered in this chapter, but some implications for the national adoption of the framework will be suggested.

Terminology is always problematic when advocating a strategy for a specific objective. The term 'mathematically promising' is a means to emphasise potential rather than the use of any clear-cut identification of a fixed group of pupils regarded as of higher calibre, in some sense. The use of the framework suggested in this chapter – provided by a key-concepts model – is based on the following particular assumptions:

- mathematically promising pupils will display certain attributes during their learning of mathematics only if the mathematics is presented to them in an appropriate way;
- the key-concepts model, it is argued, is an appropriate way in which mathematics can be presented to all children to maximise their learning;
- bearing in mind the realities of the teacher's situation of being engaged in teaching the whole class, the key-concepts model can be the basis of whole class teaching with mathematically promising pupils emerging because of their responses to providing for their curiosity.

Before considering the background which has led to the present national emphasis on provision for higher ability pupils, let us consider the insights provided by research literature into what we may observe in a child who possesses special abilities in mathematics. Krutetskii (1976), a Russian psychologist, conducted observational studies on mathematically 'gifted' pupils and provided a list of attributes which have guided many researchers ever since. Krutetskii's list of characteristics of the mathematically 'gifted' include the following:

- swiftness of reasoning;
- the ability to generalise;
- the ability to *deal with abstract concepts;*
- the ability to *notice and make use of mathematical structure;*
- the ability to memorise relationships;
- the ability to think flexibly.

Sheffield (1994), based on her study in the USA, also describes a set of 'Gifted and Talented Mathematical Behaviours' one can observe in mathematically able pupils. The following list of research-based behaviours from Sheffield provides useful pointers for observation. They are similar to many of the attributes in Krutestskii's list. According to Sheffield, mathematically promising pupils demonstrate the following:

- early and keen awareness, curiosity, and understanding about quantitative information;
- ability to perceive, visualise and generalise patterns and relationships;
- ability to reason analytically, deductively and inductively;
- ability to reverse a reasoning process and to switch methods easily but not impulsively;
- ability to work with mathematical concepts in fluent, flexible and creative ways;
- energy and persistence in solving difficult problems;
- ability to transfer learning to novel situations;
- tendency to formulate mathematical questions not just answer them;
- ability to organise and work with data in a variety of ways and to disregard irrelevant data.

For a practising teacher the above two lists will provide a basis for planning opportunities for children to demonstrate these attributes. The framework offered in this chapter will also support aspects of provision highlighted in the studies mentioned above.

Some background and signposts

From *Mathematics Counts* (The Cockcroft Report 1982) to World Class tests (QCA 2001) was a period of almost two decades of initiatives and guidance for the attention of teachers of mathematics. Prior to the publication of the Cockcroft Report, the introduction of comprehensive schools had established a degree of uniformity of institution for secondary pupils. The subsequent introduction of the National Curriculum (DES 1989) added another layer of uniformity of learning requirements – for primary as well as secondary pupils – presented in clearly crafted documents portraying levels of attainment for the guidance of teachers of the different subjects of the curriculum. References to a 'top ten per cent' of the ability range of pupils in state schools – in *Excellence in Cities* (DfEE 1999b) and QCA's World Class tests – have the appearance of being a radical initiative conceived and designed to ensure that higher ability pupils receive greater curriculum challenges and appropriate recognition of achievement not always previously offered.

What follows is a description of *ten* signposts, presented in chronological order, of policy declarations or authoritative pronouncements which have referred to the issue of provision for higher ability students; four have already been referred to in the previous paragraph. The framework for teaching mathematically promising pupils, to be outlined later, is provided by a key-concepts model. The following signposts collectively give a justification for producing the model; individually, they either support the inclusion of a specific component or provide an aspect of relevant context for the model's adoption.

The Cockcroft Report (1982) contains four paragraphs which make explicit reference to the top ten per cent, gifted children (the top two or three per cent), high-attaining children or children whose mathematical attainment is high. It declares that:

> *High attaining children should combine more rapid progress through the mathematics syllabus with more demanding work related to topics which have already been encountered.*
> (para 332)

A strategy for providing more demanding work related to topics that have already been encountered is offered by the model.

HMI (1985), in its authoritative deliberations on the mathematics curriculum, makes explicit references to two key components – **facts and skills** – placing them in a significant envelope of understanding.

They declare:

> *Pupils need to know and remember some basic mathematical facts at each level if progress is to be made with confidence, but the memory demands in mathematics can be much reduced through a sound conceptual understanding of the structure of the subject.* (p. 8)

The model will give recognition to the importance of facts. It will also take into account the HMI advice by incorporating the component isomorphism, the term for similarity of structure. The HMI's perception of the role and importance of the acquisition of skills during the process of mathematics education is an unqualified endorsement of the Cockcroft Report (1982) since it quotes from it:

> *Skills include not only the use of the number facts and the standard computational procedures of arithmetic and algebra, but also of any well established procedures which it is possible to carry out by the use of the routine. They need not only to be understood and embedded in the conceptual structure but also to be brought up to the level of immediate recall or fluency of performance by regular practice.*   (para 240)

The central importance of skills as well as the key concept of algorithm – a computational or established procedure – is endorsed as is the need to promote an appreciation of the **creativity** of mathematics. Let us remind ourselves of the words of the National Curriculum working party (DES 1988):

> *Mathematics ... should be offering pupils intellectual excitement ... and ... Pupils should also appreciate the creativity of mathematics.*   (p. 3)

In *Tackling the Mathematics Problem* the working group established by the Council of the London Mathematical Society (1995) because of concerns with the calibre of students entering mathematically based courses in higher education declared it had found 'a serious lack of essential technical facility – the ability to undertake numerical and algebraic calculation with fluency and accuracy' (p. 2). It also deplored the evidence of a changed perception of what mathematics is – in particular of the essential place within it of precision and **proof**. This supports the inclusion of 'fluency' and 'proof' in the model.

More recently, *Excellence in Schools* (DfEE 1997) put out the clarion call that

> *all schools should seek to create an atmosphere in which to excel is not only acceptable but desirable.*   (p. 39)

and two distinct, but consistent echoes came soon afterwards conveying both primary and secondary exhortations.

Excellence in Cities (DfEE 1999b) contains the requirement that 'Secondary schools will be expected to develop a distinct teaching and learning programme for their most able five to ten per cent of pupils' (p. 21) and, complementary to this, DfEE (1999a) offers the following advice for the development of teaching and learning strategies for Literacy and Mathematics:

> *In shared lessons, able pupils should have opportunities to set their own questions, offer opinions and views, interpret information and reflect and speculate on the topic.* (p. 5)

The model to follow includes **conjecture**, a specific format for mathematical questions and distinguishes three categories of information distinctive in mathematical enquiry. The contention that mathematical information is expressed in the form of natural language, in the form of the specialised symbols of mathematics or with the aid of diagrams will be explored because, it is believed, children vary in their competence to process and learn information in the three categories.

Let us get on with it is the message from Linda Sheffield, the chairperson of the US Task Force appointed to lead a group who had the responsibility for devising strategies for enhancing provision for mathematically promising pupils. Sheffield's view (1999), with regard to an appropriate curriculum for mathematically promising pupils, is unequivocal:

> *... we need to drop the old arguments of whether a program should enrich or accelerate. The model for a good mathematics program must take into consideration the depth of mathematics that is being learned.* (p. 44)

The search for depth of understanding in the quest to acquire a mathematically based view of many aspects of our world is worthy of emphasis in the teaching of mathematically promising pupils.

Those who work within mathematics education may often have an unquestioning attitude towards the intrinsic value both of mathematics and the need for all members of a population to possess a good foundation in the subject.

In the conclusion of this section and with reference to the issue of purpose relating to mathematics education, reference must be made to the report *All Our Futures* (DfEE 1999a) since it declares there is a need for a national strategy for creative and cultural education. Referring to the previously published *Excellence in Schools*, the report declares:

> *It emphasised the urgent need to unlock the potential of every young person and argued that Britain's economic prosperity and social cohesion depend on this.* (p. 6)

It may be apt here to take note of the comment of Barber (2002), in the context of launching the World Class tests:

> *World Class Tests are a key element of the UK government's strategy for gifted and talented children and will act as a benchmark to ensure that pupils educated in England are on a par with the best world-wide.* (Foreword to the book)

I have identified ten signposts plucked from two decades of the shifting sands of authoritative statements about mathematics education. It is hoped that collectively they have stimulated questions in the mind of the reader about the purpose of learning mathematics – for the individual and the nation – as well as what is entailed in guiding bright children towards the intellectual rewards of an enhanced understanding of the subject.

Schools can significantly contribute to a country's future economic prosperity by nurturing many of its most able pupils to become creative mathematicians. Before embarking on the presentation of the framework for curriculum provision for able mathematics pupils, a general issue will be briefly considered so that it may provide a background for understanding the fundamental justification for the adoption of the framework.

The logic of the strategy of 'identification and provision'

At conferences and in discussions concerning those higher ability pupils variously referred to as 'able', 'very intelligent' or 'gifted', it is quite common to call upon the twin actions of identification and provision as the key to a viable curriculum strategy. In the spirit of creativity and conjecture to be embraced by the framework, it seems pertinent to ask whether this sequence of actions – identification followed by provision – is appropriate for the development of an appropriate learning strategy for able mathematics pupils. Consider the many cases of serious underachievement with which teachers are confronted. Evidence for the underachievement is often provided by test scores, indicating that the pupil's performance in the test is less than might be expected, on average, from a pupil of such a chronological age. Much outstanding work has been done, over the years, by dedicated teachers in such cases. Yet what makes possible the teacher's task in devising an appropriate learning programme for a pupil judged to be underachieving, is the existence of a target test indicating an acceptable level of achievement for a pupil of the specified chronological age. Teachers need to consider the extent to which they agree with the previous statement and to carefully articulate to themselves the grounds for any disagreement. Now let us turn to cases of underachievement of able pupils. Of course, motivational factors could loom large in the explanation of the underachievement. Methods for the removal of any disenchantment with mathematics may involve pastoral as much as curriculum initiatives. In the present context, however, the question to be given serious consideration may be stated as follows:

The strategy of identification followed by provision has been used, with a large measure of success, for many years in relation to lower ability pupils. Is it appropriate to transfer that same sequence of activities to make satisfactory curriculum provision for pupils at the other end of the ability range? Experience in being involved with the learning of a significant number of highly intelligent pupils suggests that it is usually impossible to make accurate predictions about where they may take a learning task. This is conditional, of course, on the learning task either being originally designed or subsequently amended to enable the pupils 'to fly with it unhindered by the need to reach a pre-determined solution'.

It will, therefore, be assumed that 'identification and provision' has been an effective two-part banner enabling teachers to lead many lower ability children away from a condition of confusion and underachievement towards the satisfaction of standard progress. Let us all be glad of that! It will, however, also be assumed that many high ability pupils with unstifled creativity are more in need of teachers with a two-part pennant of curiosity and conjecture to guide them towards unanticipated ideas and explorations which they find their present apparatus of mathematical techniques to be inadequate to pursue. Far from being an unsatisfactory state of affairs, the acquisition of appropriate new knowledge and techniques can become an imperative for some very able pupils. Creating the feeling of need for new knowledge is a powerful motivating influence!

A framework for provision for higher ability mathematicians

So, the selection of signposts from two decades of pronouncements, the rejection of the two-part banner and the adoption of a two-part pennant have led to the threshold of presentation of a framework. It has been found to facilitate the grasp of the major features of the framework it is useful to present its features as a diagram. Figure 7.1 below succinctly portrays the framework's features as a pentagon within a pentagon, with all the diagonals of the outer pentagon drawn.

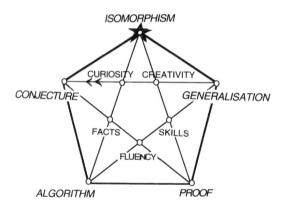

Figure 7.1   The key-concepts model

Each vertex of the inner pentagon has been given a label specifying a salient component of the learner's attributes or dispositions. Each vertex of the outer pentagon has a selected key concept assigned to it highlighting the judgement that the named concept has a key role in the development of a deep understanding of mathematics and in the design of learning tasks for able learners of mathematics. The diagonals of the outer pentagon, as will be explored later when considering examples of appropriate learning tasks, may be thought of as representing 'pathways of influence' of the outer key concepts on the inner dispositions and attributes, as well as pathways of influence – sometimes limiting – of the inner components on the outer-key concepts.

Even the sides of the pentagons may represent pathways of influence. Some examples, in advance, may help the reader and influence their path through the text.

Generalisation will require proof.

Conjecture will sometimes stimulate the search for relevant algorithms. The lines joining the pair of vertices represents the influence each may have on the other member of the pair.

Parts of the diagonals may also be considered meaningful in their representation. The line from curiosity to conjecture suggests the fundamental influence on conjecture of curiosity and creativity. Other aspects of mathematical thought – in the use of facts and skills, joined by parts of diagonals to algorithms and proof – are shown as having pathways of major influence on the ability to use algorithms and devise proofs.

At a conference presentation of the diagram the question was raised as to why pentagons were the preferred selected shapes. Since mathematics is being portrayed as an instrument for human understanding, it seems reasonable to be anthropomorphic in description of the instrument. The two sets of five vertices of the two pentagons may each be thought of as being in one-to-one correspondence with the fingers of a hand. What better way to get a grip on things!

Since the framework being presented is really a model of provision for teaching able mathematics pupils, the following issues need to be borne in mind:

- Any view of what is an appropriate method of teaching has embedded within it a view as to what is entailed in the process of learning.
- Any model is, by virtue of being a model, a simplification of the reality of a situation. Some degree of simplification is a necessary pre-requisite for understanding the subject of the model. The major advantage of any model is the guidance it provides to focus on key elements specified in the description.
- Any evaluation of the model may involve either an appraisal of its intrinsic merits, resulting in disagreement with the inclusion of one or more of its parts.
- Any attempt to use the model for presenting learning tasks to able mathematics pupils will, in large measure, require significant input from the teacher. The amount of effort on the part of the teacher is at least as important as the intrinsic soundness of the model.

The above remarks concerning the nature of models and the way in which they may be sensibly judged will, it is hoped, be helpful in grasping the detail of the model which follows. The three illustrations of the model's application to three learning tasks should provide acceptable evidence of the model's effectiveness. It is not an untried abstraction. It has been used as a basis for some schools for enhancing achievement – a number of Year 6 pupils obtaining Level 6 SATs results where previously there had been none!

Since the framework for teaching able mathematics pupils is being presented in the form of a model and the outer five components of the model are collectively referred to as key concepts, the model will be referred to as the key-concepts model. Now for sufficient detail about the components of the model to enable you to understand how it can be used with the three learning tasks later provided for illustration. After that you can try it out for yourselves!

The components of the model

The inner five components, as shown in Figure 7.1, were previously described as attributes or dispositions of the learner. The justification for their inclusion was provided in the landscape scan of two decades and the choice of meaningful signposts. It remains to give some justification for the inclusion of 'curiosity'. More on this will emerge quite naturally later when the outer five key concepts are discussed – particularly the concept of conjecture. Nevertheless, some preliminary justification could be offered at this stage, using a non-mathematical analogy. Even in the home there are, unfortunately, dangers. The label 'Keep out of reach of children' is vital as a warning. Protection from curiosity about potentially dangerous medicine is a wise precaution. The same label could be attached to lessons in school. Why protect children from their curiosity about possible answers to mathematical questions they have themselves created? Teacher directed questions have authority – in the eyes of the teacher. Child created questions have inherent interest – in the eyes of the child. Can dismissing their questions in the present kill much of their motivation in the future? Without curiosity there would be no moon landing, no DNA structure and no word processing. Curiosity for mathematical insight for the young could lead to meaningful discovery for the future.

Let us now return to a brief consideration of the five inner components of the key-concepts model.

The inner five components of the model

Facts and skills are the fundamental components, the fuel of mathematical investigation. Facts can be remembered in different forms. The basic numerical fact 'two plus five is seven' may be remembered by a child in words – in its natural language, but recorded on paper as '2+5=7'. This requires progress to have been made in the capacity to deal with a degree of abstraction. Assuming the fact has been remembered, in natural language form, without the aid of fingers, the writing of the fact using symbols beyond the list of letters of the alphabet, without writing the 2 and 5 back to front, may be viewed as an early step towards the stage of formal operations. The cognitive acceleration of some children seems well beyond what may be expected of them, considering their chronological age. Their capacity for abstraction and formal representation using the special symbolism of mathematics can be startling and could set them apart from most of their class. Other children may also be more adept, for a variety of reasons, in thinking and recording in the symbolism of mathematics. It is for such reasons that the learning and recording of facts has been found to be approachable from three different perspectives, each employing different recording mechanisms: **natural language, special symbolism and diagrams.** Note that the Pythagoreans represented numbers as dots. Take a look at a few pages of a mathematics textbook and see whether it contains the three types of representation of facts in the description of a learning task.

This approach to what is involved in communicating mathematics is very compatible with what cognitive science, in the second half of the last century, devised as a model of mental processing. A diagrammatic representation of this, an information processing model, is shown in Figure 7.2 below.

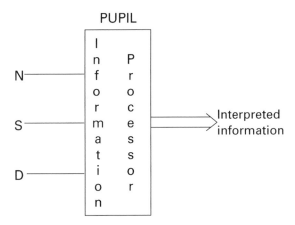

Figure 7.2   An information processing model

Note that N denotes information expressed in a natural (ordinary) language, using just the letters of an alphabet and punctuation marks; S denotes information expressed by using the special symbols of mathematics – for numbers, operations on numbers, the sign for equality and so on; D denotes information conveyed in the form of a diagram – such as a pentagon – or perhaps a picture of some kind. It is suggested that judgements relating to learning material and a pupil's learning style and competence take into account the information processing model, by consideration of questions such as:

- In what proportion does the learning material use natural language, special symbols and diagrams to define the task – be it a problem or simply a drill exercise?
- What are the relative strengths and weaknesses in the learning style of the pupil? Is there, for example, a preference to think in terms of diagrams?
- Is there, perhaps, an unusual capacity to think and write in terms of algebraic expressions, formulae and equations well beyond what one would normally expect of a child of its chronological age?

Questions to consider

The significance of this three-part system for the communication of mathematics is closely related to the two purposes of the inner five components of the model for the teacher – the assessment of the pupil and the judgement of the suitability of the learning task.

When considering whether a particular learning task is suitable for a class, group or individual child, the teacher could consider the following questions:

- What facts are needed to perform the task?
- What skills are required to engage in the task with at least some success?
- Will the facts and skills be remembered and used with sufficient fluency so as not to slow down the performance of the task?
- Will the task generate curiosity?
- Does the task have the potential to give opportunities for creativity?

The curiosity and creativity aspects have been found to be the most difficult to judge in advance. With experience, both teachers and pupils can take pleasure in unexpected learning opportunities, as the three illustrations to be described will highlight.

There are, of course, five complementary questions which may be asked of the pupils in relation to any specific learning task:

- Are the facts required for the task known?
- Have the necessary skills been acquired?
- Will the facts and skills be recalled with speed and applied with fluency?
- Will there be enough curiosity about the task for it to generate productive learning?
- Does the task have ingredients giving opportunities for displaying creativity?

Having given the ten questions some attention and taken the decision to engage the whole class, group or individual pupil in the task, there are some general points to bear in mind. Even a basic treatment of the task could give practice in the use of facts and the application of skills, thus contributing to fluency and an enhanced performance with a future task. The curiosity and creativity may be jogged by the teacher from time to time or may be self-induced by the pupil; the latter can be encouraged in a classroom atmosphere conducive to the pursuit of ideas and new knowledge.

It is hoped that enough has been said about the inner five components for them to comfortably be in one-to-one correspondence with the fingers of one of the hands of the reader's choice. It may help to re-enforce the role of the inner five if they be presented again with different anthropomorphic elements. Recall the old adage 'A healthy mind in a healthy body'. Then the five mental components may be viewed in physical terms:

> *Facts and skills are the feet on which the learning stands.*
> *Curiosity is the hormone of mental growth.*
> *Fluency is the circulation of all facts and skills.*
> *Creativity is the fitness exercise machine of the mind.*

The outer five components of the model

Now for the outline description of the outer five components – the key concepts of the model – and the possibility of them being metaphorically linked to aspects of human bondage to be relieved by mathematical learning. In one respect the description of the outer five will need to be different to that of the inner five because they are part of the technical vocabulary of mathematics. They will, therefore, each need to be introduced by means of specific mathematical example so as not to create misunderstanding when working through the three learning task illustrations later on.

Referring to Figure 7.1, you should notice two distinct markings, one on a diagonal and one at a vertex. It is useful to recall the reference to a two-part pennant, the metaphorical construct associated with the central role of the teacher as the pupil's guide towards an enhanced understanding of mathematics. Recall also the comment that the diagonals of the outer pentagon should be thought of as representing 'pathways of influence'. The double arrow-head on the section of the diagonal leading from 'curiosity' to 'conjecture' is meant to place emphasis on the central, crucial importance of conjecture in mathematics – the raising of questions and speculation about possible connections between things and its ultimate dependence on the curiosity of the learner. Without curiosity there is no interesting question worth pursuing! The role of the teacher may be symbolically represented as that of waving the two-part pennant encouraging children along the pathway from curiosity to conjecture. The star placed on the vertex labelled 'isomorphism' is meant to emphasise the view that discovering that two things or situations have the same underlying structure – the essence of the notion of isomorphism – is a pinnacle of achievement for the learner of mathematics.

So, let us now go through the list of five key concepts of the model in order, giving examples to convey their meanings. It is hoped that further understanding of how the five concepts emerge during the performance of a learning task – to be illustrated by going through three tasks – will give sufficient appreciation of how the model may be used to enable the reader to use it with other tasks so as to lead either a whole class or an individual pupil from curiosity to isomorphism.

Illustration of the key concepts

The simplest examples will be used to illustrate each of the key concepts. Let us start with the fundamental 'conjecture'. Basic additions of integers (whole numbers) are being carried out.

$$6 + 8 = 14 \text{ and } 5 + 11 = 16.$$

The pupil notices that the sum (answer) is always even and conjectures that when you add two integers the sum is always even. Looking for exceptions to a rule or what seems to be a general result is a procedure worth encouraging; it can prevent 'jumping to conclusions' and declaring generalisations to be true without good cause. All that needs to be tried in this case is the addition of 8 and 9 giving 17, an odd number. So the conjecture was too hasty. Further carefully selected pairs of integers could lead to the conjecture:

Is the sum of two integers always even unless one of them is even and the other is odd?

Trying several more pairs of integers could make the pupil very confident in what had been discovered about adding two integers. So much so that the pupil asserts the generalisation:

The sum of two integers is always even unless one of them is even and the other is odd.

A generalisation is a statement which is always true without exception. Another generalisation, from Euclidean geometry, is:

The sum of the three angles of a triangle is 180 degrees.

This is true of any triangle; there is no triangle with three angles which do not add up to 180 degrees. Curiosity, then, has led to a conjecture and that has led to a generalisation. The pupil may be convinced, but the truth of what has been found about the addition of integers has not yet been proved. A proof can sometimes be given in just natural language – that is, in words only. More often, however, a proof needs to be given using the special symbols of mathematics – that is, algebraically. A proof of the above generalisation about the addition of two integers could be presented as follows:

> Let an even integer be $2n$. This is how an even integer is defined, as a double of an unspecified integer n. Let $2m$ be another even integer.
> Let an odd integer be $2n + 1$. This is how an odd integer is defined, as a double plus one. Let $2m + 1$ be another odd integer.
> Then $2n + 2m = 2(n + m)$, which is even because $2(n + m)$ is the double of $(n + m)$.
> Also, $(2n + 1) + (2m + 1) = 2(n + m + 1)$ which is even because $2(n + m + 1)$ ia the double of $(n + m + 1)$.
> However, $2n + (2m + 1) = 2(n + m) + 1$, which is odd because it is the double of $(n + m)$ plus one.
> Therefore, the sum of two integers is even unless one of them is even and the other is odd.
> This completes the proof.

It should be emphasised that in mathematical proof, as opposed to a court of law, what has been proved must be certainly true, given the truth of the assumptions, rather than true beyond reasonable doubt given the evidence.

The next key concept, the notion of algorithm, should be more familiar, since it is a central part of teaching mathematics. An algorithm is just a step-by-step procedure for completing something like addition or subtraction. So every child needs to know four algorithms, one for carrying out each of the operations of addition, subtraction, multiplication and division. There is no need to dwell on this.

Standard algorithms do need to be learnt, together with the fluency and skill in using them. Yet there are times when a child may be smart enough to try an easier way of doing something, rather than plod through the algorithm already learnt. The operation of subtraction provides an easy illustration. Suppose a child need to subtract 47 from 2005. The standard algorithm requiring the units to be written in the rightmost column and the tens in the column to the left causes difficulty for many, because of the two zeros. A smart child could well opt for what it considers to be an easier algorithm, based on the notion of a number line. The child could draw or imagine the diagram below.

Figure 7.3

Then the child could proceed, by thinking as follows:

> From 47 to 100 is 53.
> From 100 to 2000 is 1900. 53 added to 1900 is 1953. Add another 5 to give 1958. It works. The activity of finding alternative algorithms which are sometimes easier and more efficient, is part of creativity and should not be discouraged.

Now for the fifth, last and in a way the most important of the key concepts – isomorphism, similarity of structure. In a world where so many adults are intent on seeing differences between things which are similar, why not guide children towards seeing similarity between things which superficially appear different!

Let us try understanding isomorphism by means of an example. Think of one situation in which a sergeant is drilling soldiers to march on a parade ground. Think of another situation in which a car driver is undertaking a journey being navigated by a passenger. The two situations can be thought of as isomorphic and be mathematically represented in the same way. How can this be justified?

Assume the following. When the driver of the car starts the journey, the car is parked pointing north. When the sergeant starts his drill, the soldiers are facing a statue at the end of the parade ground. So the statue is similar to the north direction.

The passenger of the car gives only the instructions:

> START
> STOP
> Turn left
> Turn right
> Do a 3-point turn

The last instruction would be needed to go back the way they had come because they had missed a turning.

The sergeant on the parade ground gives only the following instructions:

> QUICK MARCH
> HALT
> Left turn
> Right turn
> About turn

The sergeant's instructions, considered in the order listed, are similar to the passenger's instructions, considered in the order in which they were listed above. It is this similarity which gives the two situations their isomorphism. This ability to see the similarity between two seemingly different situations can be of importance in problem solving. A further advantage of the detection of isomorphism depends on the possibility of creating the same mathematical method to represent the two situations. One way of demonstrating the similarity of the above two situations would be to use four numbers and the symbol for addition, as follows:

0 represents facing or heading north;
90 represents facing or heading east;
180 represents facing or heading south;
270 represents facing or heading west.

(Turning left can be thought of as being the same as turning clockwise through 270 degrees. The 'facing' and 'heading' options are interchangeable.)

Imagine the soldiers or the car driver following the instructions given by the following mathematical expression:

90 + 270 + 180 + 90 + 90.

Which way are they facing when they have finished? You could go through it by thinking of 'turn right', 'turn left', '3-point turn', 'turn right' and 'turn right' again. The soldiers would be facing the statue or the car would be facing north.

Alternately, the end result could be decided by adding the numbers, subtracting 360 whenever 360 or more is obtained. The result is 0, as expected. Other examples could be tried using the table below.

Second instruction

	+	0	90	180	270
	0	0	90	180	270
	90	90	180	270	0
	180	180	270	0	90
	270	270	0	90	180

First instruction

Figure 7.4

So, there you are. The description of the key-concepts model is complete.

Is there a way of remembering the outer five components, using some kind of anthropomorphic analogy? Well, let us think. List the words: Conjecture,

Isomorphism, Generalisation, Proof, Algorithm. Take their first letters. C,I,G,P,A. Is an anagram of the five possible? There are 5 times 4 times 3 times 2 times 1 possibilities. That comes to 120 anagrams. The best seems to be PAGIC. At least that is closer to MAGIC than PATHETIC which is not even an option. One last thought on the matter:

Perspiration And Guts Inevitably Conquer.

Any chance of that becoming the class motto for mathematics lessons? The time has come to illustrate how the key-concepts model can provide guidance through the performance of a learning task. Should you find the going gets a bit rough, you may find the motto quite useful.

Exemplification of key concepts – Task 1

The first task is selected from DfEE (2000a) and is entitled 'Three digits'. It is shown in full in Figure 7.5.

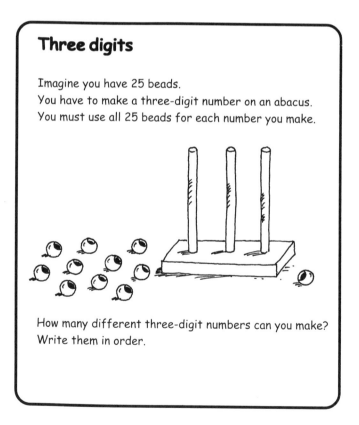

Three digits

Imagine you have 25 beads.
You have to make a three-digit number on an abacus.
You must use all 25 beads for each number you make.

How many different three-digit numbers can you make?
Write them in order.

Figure 7.5   A mathematical challenge

The two-pennant banner 'Curiosity and Conjecture' can take curiosity for granted, since a class or pupil is assumed to be trying it. The conjecture is given as the question in the task description.

The facts and skills needed relate to a knowledge of place value, the skill to write three-digit numbers with fluency and to add three integers to check the total is 25. The creativity required is the systematic approach and recording which will lead to the solution of the problem. The recording of the solution could be as follows:

> Express 25 as the sum of three digits.
> The first digit could be 1,2,3…9
> The second digit could be 1,2,3…9
> The third digit could be 1,2,3…9

Being systematic in recording the possibilities would produce the following:

> 9,9,7
> 9,9,8
> 9,7,9
> 9,6 – Not possible
> 8,9,8
> 8,8,9
> 8,7 – Not possible
> 7,9,9
> 7,8 – Not possible

Therefore, there are three possible numbers starting with 9: 997, 998 and 979. There are two possible numbers starting with 8: 898 and 889. Lastly there is just one possible number starting with 7: 799. That makes 3 + 2 + 1 = 6 possible numbers.

That is the end of the task as given. Yet the 'Curiosity–Conjecture' banner, supported by PAGIC could take things much further.

Several conjectures could arise from an able mathematician's curiosity:

> Is there a connection between the number of beads and the total possible numbers which can be made?
> What other number of beads will give 3 + 2 + 1 = 6 possible three-digit numbers?
> Is there a number of beads which will give:
> 2 + 1 = 3 possible three-digit numbers?
> 4 + 3 + 2 + 1 = 10 possible three-digit numbers?

Since 25 beads were investigated, let us consider 26 beads. With 26 beads you can make 998, 989 and 899. There are, then, 2 + 1 = 3 possible three-digit numbers. With 27 beads only 999 is possible, just 1. Using more than 27 beads is not possible because a maximum of 9 can be placed on each rod. Having explored three-digit numbers with 27, 26 and 25 beads, what about 1, 2 and 3 beads? These give 100 for one bead; 200, 110 and 101 for two beads; 300, 210, 201, 120, 102 and 111 for three beads. There is now a generalisation emerging with a creative look at the results so far. The number of possible three-digit numbers which can be made with 27 is the same as with 1; the same is possible with 26 and 2; the same is possible with 25 and 3. The pair of numbers of beads totals 28 each time. This leads to the conjecture that 24 beads will give the same result as 4 beads. Testing this produces ten three-digit numbers for 24 as well as 4. It is also noteworthy that $10 = 4 + 3 + 2 + 1$. The sum of the consecutive integers keeps cropping up. This is a good opportunity to try a proof before further exploration. So, let S denote the sum of the first n integers. Then $S = 1 + 2 + 3 + \ldots + n$. (The three dots stand for all the missing integers between 3 and n). Changing the order produces:

$$S = n + (n - 1) + (n - 2) + \ldots + 1$$

Adding the two forms of S together gives:

$$2S = (n + 1) \; n \text{ times.}$$

This proves that $S = n/2(n + 1)$. In case you are wondering, there are definitely Key Stage 2 pupils who can cope with this.

If curiosity and PAGIC still have an influence, further insight is more likely to occur if the results obtained up to this point are recorded in a table, with some more included which you may care to check.

Number of beads	Possible three-digit numbers	
27	1	= 1
26	3	= 1 + 2
25	6	= 1 + 2 + 3
24	10	= 1 + 2 + 3 + 4
23	15	= 1 + 2 + 3 + 4 + 5
5	15	= 1 + 2 + 3 + 4 + 5
4	10	= 1 + 2 + 3 + 4
3	6	= 1 + 2 + 3
2	3	= 1 + 2
1	1	= 1

The results displayed give strong support to a generalisation. The number of beads which may be used to represent three-digit numbers may range from 1 to

27, but two amounts which add up to 28 will always give the same number of three-digit numbers. Following on from this are two conjectures. The number of three-digit numbers which can be represented using 15 beads is the same as for 13 beads. This number is 91, the sum of the first 13 integers. 14 beads gives the maximum number of three-digit numbers, which is 105. That is enough for the purpose of exploring what can be done with this particular learning task.

Exemplification of key concepts – Task 2

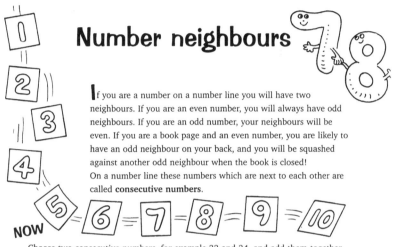

Number neighbours

If you are a number on a number line you will have two neighbours. If you are an even number, you will always have odd neighbours. If you are an odd number, your neighbours will be even. If you are a book page and an even number, you are likely to have an odd neighbour on your back, and you will be squashed against another odd neighbour when the book is closed!
On a number line these numbers which are next to each other are called **consecutive numbers**.

NOW

Choose two consecutive numbers, for example 33 and 34, and add them together. Choose another pair of consecutive numbers and add them together. Add some more. Is there a pattern? Write down what you have noticed in a bubble.

Try adding three consecutive numbers, for example 27, 28 and 29. Add another set of three consecutive numbers. What have you noticed? Write this down in another bubble. Does your theory take into account whether you started with an odd number or an even number? You must have already made some discoveries.

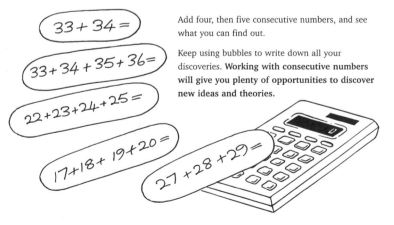

Add four, then five consecutive numbers, and see what you can find out.

Keep using bubbles to write down all your discoveries. **Working with consecutive numbers will give you plenty of opportunities to discover new ideas and theories.**

$33 + 34 =$

$33 + 34 + 35 + 36 =$

$22 + 23 + 24 + 25 =$

$17 + 18 + 19 + 20 =$

$27 + 28 + 29 =$

Figure 7.6   'Number neighbours' activity from Casey and Koshy (1995)

Some attention has previously been given to the addition of two consecutive numbers. The facts and skills required for the task are a knowledge of at least two-digit numbers and fluency in the use of the algorithm for addition, with three-digit totals sometimes needing to be recorded. There is substantial scope for generalisation and proof in working on this task.

A pupil could try two groups of three consecutive, one starting with an even number and the other starting with an odd number.

20 + 21 + 22 = 63, an odd number.
37 + 38 + 39 = 114, an even number.

This suggests the conjecture that the sum of three consecutive numbers is odd when the first number is even and even when the first number is odd. An able mathematics pupil could well dispense with trials and devise a proof of the generalisation incorporated in the conjecture.

So, consider the sum of $2n$, $2n + 1$ and $2n + 2$. It comes to $6n + 3$. This is odd because $6n + 3 = 2(3n + 1) + 1$; the double of $3n + 1$ is even and adding 1 to that produces an odd number. Hence the sum of three consecutive numbers is odd when the first of the numbers is even. Similarly, for the next part of the proof.

The sum of $2m + 1$, $2m + 2$ and $2m + 3$ is $6m + 6$, which is the double of $3m + 3$. This has proved the sum of three consecutive numbers is even when the first of the numbers is odd. Generalisations and proofs for four and for five consecutive numbers may be produced along the same lines. Curiosity and stamina determine how far a pupil will pursue the ideas involved.

Exemplification of key concepts – Task 3

The third and last of the illustrations of how the key-concepts model can guide a class or pupil through a task will focus on the all important concept of isomorphism.

The task is described in the following two paragraphs.

A football tournament is to be arranged between five teams, so that every team must play every other team once only. How many matches need to be arranged and played? Assume that the teams are Newcastle, Ipswich, Derby, Blackburn and Southampton.

A transport minister has decided that each of five towns needs to be directly linked to each of the other towns by newly built roads. How many new roads need to be built? Assume that the towns are Grimsby, Hastings, Newport, Plymouth and Stockport.

The facts and skills needed for this task include the ability to add consecutive numbers and the creativity to devise a recording system which reveals the isomorphism of the two situations.

The first situation is represented by Figure 7.7. An arc is drawn from one dot to another to represent a match arranged between the corresponding teams.

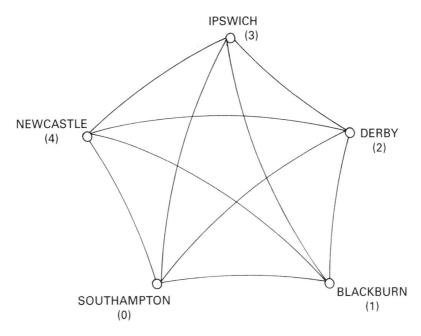

Figure 7.7 The first situation

To avoid double counting, as the matches are decided for a team, starting with Newcastle, the number of newly arranged matches is written near the dot representing the team. So, working clockwise, when it comes to Blackburn only 1 new match needs to be arranged. Hence the number of matches that need to be organised is $4 + 3 + 2 + 1$, which is 10. Once again, the sum of the integers starting with 1 has arisen.

If the diagram for the football problem is changed so that Newcastle is replaced by Grimsby, Ipswich by Hastings, Derby by Newport, Blackburn by Plymouth and Southampton by Stockport, then the solution to the second problem follows from the diagram in exactly the same way as before. Figure 7.8 shows the representation for the road construction problem.

The two situations are isomorphic and the two diagrams, considered together, reveal and display the similarity of structure.

A few comments may be made to conclude the account of how the key concepts model may be used, both to judge the requirements of a learning task and to extend it when appropriate with inserted conjectures.

A specific learning task may generate work on some key concepts much more than others; sometimes a concept may not be involved at all.

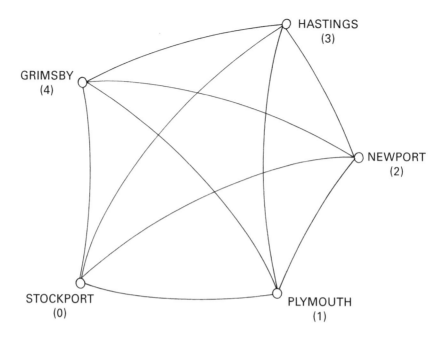

Figure 7.8   The second situation

Most learning tasks may be started as whole-class activities and then involve fewer and fewer pupils as more and more conjectures are explored as they arise from the curiosity of either the pupils or the teacher.

Concluding remarks

Finally, may I commend the key-concepts model to you. It has been tried by pupils, classes and teachers. The future evaluations of its usefulness will depend on the dedicated efforts of teachers and the extent to which they have got a grip on the inner and outer five components. The 'Curiosity–Conjecture' pennant is in their hands. It is earnestly hoped that it will make some contribution to the emergence of creative, young mathematicians and to future economic prosperity.

References

Barber, M.(2002) Forward to *Assessing Gifted and Talented Children*. London: QCA.

Casey, R. and Koshy,V. (1995) *Bright Challenge*. Available from Valsa Koshy, Brunel University, 300 St Margaret's Road, Twickenham TW1 1PT.

Cockcroft, W. H. (1982) *Mathematics Counts. Report of the Committee of inquiry into the Teaching of Mathematics in Schools*. London: HMSO.

DES (1988) *Mathematics for Ages 5 to 16. Proposals to the Secretary of State for Education and Science.* London: HMSO.

DES (1989) *Mathematics in the National Curriculum.* London: HMSO.

DfEE (1997) *Excellence in Schools.* London: DfEE.

DfEE(1999a) *All our Futures. Creativity, Culture and Education.* London: DfEE.

DfEE (1999b) *Excellence in Cities.* London: DfEE.

DfEE (2000a) *Mathematical Challenges for able pupils in Key Stages 1 and 3.* London: DfEE.

DfEE (2000b) *National Literacy and Numeracy Strategies: Guidance on Teaching Able Children.* London: DfEE.

HMI (1985) *Mathematics 5–16: Curriculum Matters 3.* London: HMSO.

Krutetskii. V. A. (1976) *The Psychology of Mathematical Abilities in School Children.* Chicago, Ill.: University of Chicago Press.

QCA (2001) Information on World Class tests can be obtained form website www.worldclassarena.org

The London Mathematical Society (1995) *Tackling the Mathematics Problem.* London: LMS.

Sheffield, L. (1994) *The Development of Gifted and Talented Mathematics Students and the National Council of Teachers of Mathematics Standards.* Connecticut: The National Research Centre on the Gifted and Talented.

Sheffield, L. (1999) 'Serving the Needs of the Mathematically Promising', in Sheffield, L. (ed.) *Developing Mathematically promising students.* Reston, Va.: NCTM.

CHAPTER 8

Assessing mathematical learning

VALSA KOSHY

Teachers have always assessed children's learning in a variety of ways. Classroom assessment may take place as informal or structured observations or as written tests. Whatever method of assessment is used, the main purpose of assessment remains the same – to provide information about children's learning. During a recent in-service session I asked teachers how they would define assessment. They felt that in spite of their familiarity with the word 'assessment' the task of producing a definition was too complex. I then asked them to list what they thought were the most important elements of classroom assessment. The following list emerged as a set of what is involved in assessing children. Assessment involves or should involve:

- collecting information on what and how children learn;
- keeping an ongoing record of what is learnt in order to plan the next step;
- gathering information which helps to compare performances of groups of children;
- collection of data showing what the child knows and understands;
- giving feedback based on continuous observation of children's learning.

Although many changes have been introduced in school assessment since the publication of the TGAT report *National Curiculum Task Group for Assessment and Testing* (DES 1987), I felt encouraged that the lists offered by the teachers had many of the aspects included in the TGAT definition:

> *Promoting children's learning is a principal aim of schools. Assessment lies at the heart of this process. It can provide a framework in which educational objectives may be set, and pupils progress charted and expressed. It can yield a basis for planning the next educational steps in response to children's needs.* (paragraph 3)

In this chapter my aim is to explore the following questions:

1. **What is the purpose of assessment?**
2. **What does recent research tell us about the role of assessment in enhancing the quality of children's learning?**

3. What are we assessing in mathematics?
4. How do we translate the principles into classroom practice?

I will attempt to explore the above questions with examples either from my own experience or from what I have seen and know to be judged as 'good practice' in assessment.

Purposes of assessing mathematical learning

When considering classroom assessment, it is useful to explore the two main types of assessment. They are: **formative** and **summative** assessment.

Formative assessment

The purpose of formative assessment is to provide ongoing information on children's learning, enabling teachers to identify their strengths and any aspects of their learning requiring attention. The information collected helps the teacher when planning the next step in a child's learning or in deciding what action needs to be taken. In this dynamic process the teacher can give timely, useful feedback to the children and help them to set and monitor meaningful targets. The evidence gathered during formative assessment will also help the teacher to match learning material to the potential of the children and plan any remedial action needed. We assess children's day-to-day learning in the following ways.

- **By listening to what children say.** This may be during their individual conversations with the teacher, in group and class discussions. It may be informal or though structured interviews or be focused on particular instances through targeted questioning.
- **By observing what children do.** This may be in the context of children counting a set of objects or performing an algorithm and selecting the steps within a calculation. Or it may be based on the decisions they make when solving a mathematical problem. Through observation a teacher can pick up much useful information about children's knowledge, skills and gaps in their understanding of concepts. Valuable information about children's attitudes towards different tasks and to the subject of mathematics itself can be gathered during classroom observations.
- **By analysing written work.** This may happen when the teacher is marking the work or sharing their work with individual children. What children record on paper can provide significant insights into the strategies and procedures they use for calculations. Spending two or three minutes with children

who have made mistakes provides the teacher with some understanding of their way of thinking and helps her judge whether they hold any misconceptions.

All the ways of assessing described above help the teacher to build up an effective formative system which is an ongoing, day-to-day collection of information. This is different from the summative assessment carried out at the end of a term, end of a year or the end of a Key Stage.

Summative assessment

Summative assessment provides overall evidence of children's learning at a particular time. Information gathered from summative assessment is often used for selecting pupils for programmes or entry into schools and for the purpose of comparisons. League tables are constructed from the results of summative tests. Results from summative tests are also often used for evaluative purposes: to evaluate teaching methods and any general trends in children's achievement so that professional development and resources can be directed appropriately. Refined teaching strategies may also be considered so as to help to improve children's performance.

Benefits of formative assessment

In this chapter my main emphasis is on formative assessment. Although good formative assessment will inevitably improve the outcomes of summative assessment, the thrust of this chapter is to consider ways in which teachers can enhance their skills in formative assessment.

My decision to focus on formative assessment is based on my belief that it is the day-to-day judgements on children's learning and how we respond to them that can make a real difference. Before drawing on research evidence about how formative assessment can help to raise achievement, I will try to make the distinction between the roles of summative and formative assessment clear by using an analogy. Think about a parent caring for a child. From a very early age, a child is taken to a health clinic and, if necessary, to a doctor where he or she is measured using all sorts of criteria in order to assess whether his or her physical and mental development is within the normal range. If this is not the case, then prompt action is taken. This is done at different stages in a child's life and is a necessary process, but this alone will not help the child to develop. This is similar to the role of summative assessment – useful, necessary but not enough. Parents also watch their children every day, feed them, keep them warm and comfortable and take note of their ups and downs, anxieties and worries as and when they manifest themselves. It is this everyday ongoing care that helps the children feel secure and confident and plays a vital role in their growth and development. This ongoing care is similar to the role of formative assessment that enables a teacher to act before it is too late to help to enhance the children's achievement.

The role of formative assessment in raising achievement – research findings

Based on an extensive survey of research findings, Black and William (1999) listed five key factors (described by them as 'deceptively simple') that improve learning through assessment:

- the provision of effective feedback to pupils;
- the active involvement of pupils in their own learning ;
- adjusting teaching to take account of the results of assessment;
- a recognition of the profound influence assessment has on the motivation and self-esteem of pupils, both of which are crucial influences on learning;
- the need for pupils to be able assess themselves and understand how to improve.   (p. 4)

In the context of assessment of learning, they also summarise the characteristics that promote learning. These are applicable to all learning but are particularly relevant in the light of the contents of this chapter, which focuses on the role of assessment, leading to the effective learning of mathematics. The following conditions enhance learning opportunities:

- sharing learning goals with pupils;
- helping pupils to know and to recognise the standard they are aiming for;
- involving pupils in self-assessment;
- providing feedback, which leads to pupils recognising their next steps and how to take them.   (p. 7)

Research points to the following being among the factors inhibit student progress:

- a tendency for teachers to assess the quantity of work and presentation rather than the quality of learning;
- greater attention given to marking and grading, much of it tending to lower the self-esteem of pupils, rather than to providing advice for improvement; a strong emphasis on comparing pupils with each other which demoralises the less successful learners.   (p. 5)

I feel it is appropriate to conclude this section by drawing attention to what is considered important in teachers assessing pupils' work for Ofsted (2000) inspections:

> *Your judgements about teachers' assessment of their pupils should focus on how well teachers look for gains in learning, gaps in knowledge and areas of misunderstanding, through their day-to-day work with pupils. This will include marking, questioning individuals and plenary sessions. Clues to the effectiveness of formative assessment are how well the teachers listen and respond to pupils, encourage and, where appropriate, praise them, recognise and handle misconceptions, build on their responses and steer them towards clearer understanding. Effective teachers encourage pupils to judge the success of their own work and set targets for improvement. They will take full account of the targets set out in individual education plans for pupils with special educational needs.*

What are we assessing in mathematics?

A good starting point for consideration before we carry out assessment is to ask ourselves two all-important questions: **What is mathematics?** and **What are our objectives in teaching mathematics?**

Drawing on a very illuminating discussion of these by Ernest (2000), which also takes into account the objectives of teaching mathematics stated in the Cockcroft Report (1982) and HMI (1985), I will discuss the practical implications of assessing the different objectives. We need to assess whether children:

- know their mathematics facts;
- have acquired mathematical skills;
- have developed a robust conceptual understanding of mathematical ideas;
- can employ effective strategies for problem solving in mathematics;
- have positive attitudes towards the subject.

These are discussed in the following section.

Assessing facts

What are mathematical facts? Children need to learn the correct names of numbers and shapes and mathematical terms such as multiplication and fraction. They need to recognise mathematical symbols such as $+$, $-$, $\%$ and so on. Recall of number bonds such as $8 + 6 = 14$ or $7 \times 5 = 35$ is important too. These are important as they are 'the basic atoms of knowledge which fit into a larger and more meaningful system of facts' (Ernest 2000). There are many opportunities during the mathematics lesson when the acquisition of facts can be assessed. For example, during a mental starter or plenary session, we can ask targeted questions that will highlight any gaps in children's recall and recognition of facts. You could organise 'fact books' and ask children to record their number facts on a teaching topic regularly and take any action necessary. When we assess knowledge it is important to remember that a child who can recite multiplication tables correctly, or read numbers accurately, does not necessary understand the principles behind the facts or how they have been arrived at. In order to assess, we will need to gather more evidence through different kinds of questions which elicit explanations.

Assessing skills

The Cockcroft Report (1982) describes skills as an integral part of learning mathematics:

> *Skills include not only the use of the number facts and the standard computational procedures of arithmetic and algebra, but also of any well established procedures which it is possible to carry out by the use of a routine. They need not only to be understood and embedded in the conceptual structure but also to be brought up to the level of immediate recall or fluency of performance by regular practice.*   (para 240)

Performing calculations, measuring using a ruler or a protractor require the use of learnt skills. Observing children at work or listening to them verbalise their methods during a lesson or at a plenary session provides valuable insights into their ways of thinking. The steps they take or the mistakes they make can often show the teacher any patterns of misunderstandings and misconceptions. Observations can also show whether children are adopting the most sensible and efficient strategies to carry out calculations. An important point to remember here is that many of children's mistakes originate from misunderstood rules. Or they could be the result of children constructing their own set of rules without understanding the basic principles. Mistakes and misconceptions can often be corrected easily if action is taken promptly. Look at the following examples of some common mistakes children make and ask yourself: if these mistakes are spotted while marking children's work, what information do they give as to a child's competence with the particular skills? It is useful to also consider what action should be taken.

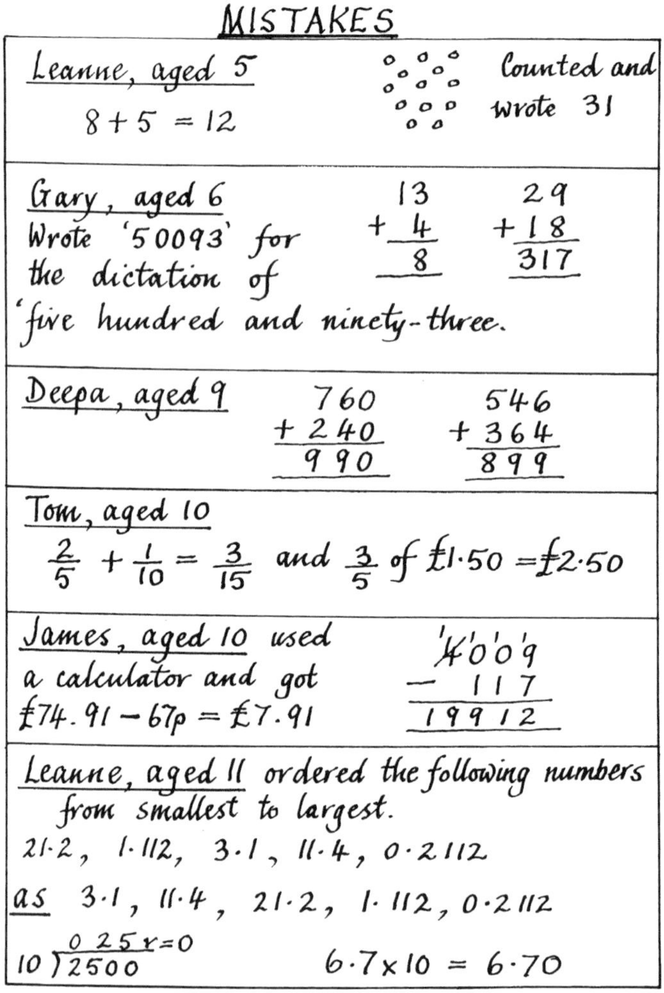

MISTAKES

Leanne, aged 5 $8 + 5 = 12$	°°°°° Counted and °°°° wrote 31

Grary, aged 6
Wrote '50093' for
the dictation of
'five hundred and ninety-three.

$$\begin{array}{r} 13 \\ +\ 4 \\ \hline 8 \end{array} \qquad \begin{array}{r} 29 \\ +18 \\ \hline 317 \end{array}$$

Deepa, aged 9

$$\begin{array}{r} 760 \\ +240 \\ \hline 990 \end{array} \qquad \begin{array}{r} 546 \\ +364 \\ \hline 899 \end{array}$$

Tom, aged 10

$$\frac{2}{5} + \frac{1}{10} = \frac{3}{15} \text{ and } \frac{3}{5} \text{ of } £1{\cdot}50 = £2{\cdot}50$$

James, aged 10 used
a calculator and got
$£74.91 - 67p = £7.91$

$$\begin{array}{r} {}^{1}4'0'0'9 \\ -\ 117 \\ \hline 19912 \end{array}$$

Leanne, aged 11 ordered the following numbers
from smallest to largest.
21·2, 1·112, 3·1, 11·4, 0·2112

as 3·1, 11·4, 21·2, 1·112, 0·2112

$$10\overline{)2500} \quad \begin{array}{l} 0\ 25\ r=0 \end{array} \qquad 6{\cdot}7 \times 10 = 6{\cdot}70$$

Figure 8.1   Examples of children's mistakes

I have attempted, elsewhere, a comprehensive discussion of children's mistakes and misconceptions in mathematics (Koshy 2000), which may provide further illumination of how analysing mistakes can contribute to formative assessment of mathematical learning.

Assessing conceptual understanding

Conceptual structures are described in the Cockcroft Report (1982) as 'richly interconnecting bodies of knowledge'. A robust conceptual understanding is necessary for children to become competent mathematicians. The HMI (1985) explains the importance of the interrelationships between concepts:

No concept stands alone: for example, subtraction is linked with addition, multiplication is linked with addition and division, percentages are linked with fractions and decimals. In fact, each concept is linked with many other aspects of mathematics ... Indeed being good at mathematics is dependent of the ability to recognise relationships between one concept and another. (p.15)

Research carried out at Kings College (Askew *et al.* 1997) also suggests that effective teachers of numeracy emphasise the interconnections between concepts. As conceptual structures grow and strengthen as the child learns more mathematics, there is a need for assessing if there are any gaps in her/his understanding of concepts and whether action needs to be taken. Where a child exhibits knowledge of facts or skills, it is not always easy to evaluate whether what has been learnt has been superficial or learnt by rote. Assessment of conceptual understanding may take longer than the assessment of facts and skills (although successful performance will depend on the acquisition of the former). For example, it is relatively easier to assess if a child recognises a number name, or the terms 'hundreds' 'tens' and 'units' than to assess if she or he understands the principle of place value. Similarly, it takes more careful assessment to recognise the nature of the difficulty experienced by a child in understanding that 9 in the hundred position represents 900. Assessing conceptual understanding needs closer observation and a good deal of probing. The role of probing questions in assessment is described, in more detail, later in this chapter.

Assessing problem-solving strategies

To become a good mathematician one needs to be an efficient problem solver and be able to undertake investigations with confidence. Development of mathematical processes such as making decisions, reasoning, working systematically, communicating ideas and generalising must form an integral part of mathematics teaching. Assessing a child's competence in problem-solving strategies is more challenging as the skills needed are not easily measurable. Assessment of problem-solving skills will involve setting up of contexts and situations in which the use of these processes can be observed. This may be time consuming, but worthwhile. Getting children to record their thoughts and methods in mathematical journals or diaries is one effective method of gathering evidence. Observing individual or group problem-solving activities and encouraging children to share their strategies with other children will also provide the teacher with opportunities for assessing this aspect of learning.

Assessing positive attitudes

Attitudes towards mathematics, such as confidence to tackle work, motivation, enjoyment and persistence are important ingredients in the effective learning of mathematics. It is often tempting, in the midst of competing priorities in the classroom, to overlook the assessment of this aspect. But the assessment of attitudes does not have to be separately organised. Observation of children carrying out their mathematical tasks, the unsolicited comments they make during the introduction or conclusion of an activity and their recordings can often provide valuable information about attitudes. Occasionally, however, asking children to record their views on a completed task and their perceptions of what and how they are learning can be extremely helpful in judging their level of motivation, especially in the light of many adults turning off the subject or even hating it later in life.

Principles to practice

The process of assessment is strongly linked to aspects of teaching and learning. The planning–teaching–learning cycle (Mitchell and Koshy 1995) shows that it is an ongoing dynamic with no specific starting point; they are interlinked.

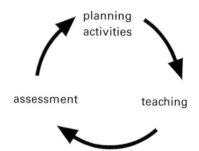

Figure 8.2 The teaching–learning–assessing cycle adapted from Mitchell and Koshy 1995

How does the cycle work in practice in the classroom? What are the implications? How can we ensure that our organisation of the planning and teaching stages contributes to effective mathematics learning?

The planning stage

At the planning stage, it is important to identity clear objectives for teaching whether it is to teach a single session or the programme for a whole term. The objectives are then translated into clear learning objectives against which assessment can be made. Of course, no assessment methods, however effectively used, will provide the teacher with a full picture of the effectiveness of what has been learnt. For example, some skills or concepts may have been learnt, but there be only partial understanding of what was taught. You could make a note of these in the plans for future reference. Then, there is all the information you collect on unexpected outcomes – the child may already have a higher level of understanding of some ideas than you expected or have more gaps in her or his knowledge than you had assessed previously. In spite of the above practical complexities one may encounter, the quality of your assessment is always enhanced if you and the children share an understanding of what the expected outcomes are for the planned lesson.

During planning of a teaching session and the listing of activities, attention should be paid to two more aspects. First, as far as possible, you must take into account any information collected previously and make any necessary adjustments to what and how the lesson is to be taught. These notes have probably been annotated in the previous plan or elsewhere for ready reference. Secondly, it is useful to consider any mistakes or misconceptions experienced by individual children or the whole class with a particular concept or skill. Being pro-active in anticipating and addressing misconceptions during the planning stage, should help the teaching of a particular topic or idea and should help the children making those mistakes or have the misconceptions. I have personal experience of this. When I shared with children mathematical ideas that had been found difficult by other children (not from the same class) using samples of their mistakes, not only did the children seem very amused by the mistakes, they tried to seek a rationale for such mistakes. I felt this process very worthwhile in enhancing children's conceptual understanding of the ideas I tried to teach.

The teaching stage

It was highlighted previously, on the basis of research findings, that sharing clearly the learning outcomes with the children helps them to:

- share the responsibility for learning;
- maintain attention for longer periods;
- stay focused when explanations are given;
- develop a framework for assessing their own learning;
- know the nature of any support needed;
- reflect on their achievement;
- become more effective contributors during target setting.

A word of caution here. Since the National Numeracy Strategy was introduced, most teachers start the lessons telling the children what the learning outcomes are to be either verbally or sometimes using an overhead transparency. One must not assume that this process alone guarantees all the benefits I have listed above. On some occasions when I have asked children during a lesson what they were learning, there has been a very clear correlation between the level of clarity with which the learning outcomes had been shared and how focused they were on their tasks. I have also found that where teachers have explained the learning outcomes with explanations and examples of what they meant, children's understanding of what was expected of them was clearer. One particular example comes to mind. Robert, an infant teacher, gave his pupils a photocopied list of learning outcomes. Then he not only explained what these meant, he also told them the kind of questions he would ask. On this specific occasion Robert's learning outcomes included learning the order in which two-digit numbers were placed on a number line. He told them that one of the tasks he would be asking them to do at the end of the lesson would be to order a set of numbers which had got muddled in their pack.

Enhancing the quality of assessment in the classroom

Here we need to remind ourselves of the two types of assessment we carry out in schools: summative and formative. The distinction between the two was explored earlier in this chapter.

The purpose of summative assessment of mathematical learning is to assess longer-term learning. This is usually carried out either at the end of term or end of year. The information gathered during summative assessment is used to:

- check whether the key objectives for the term or year are met;
- assess whether the level of achievement matches the expected outcomes;
- summarise achievements for the next teacher;
- report to parents;
- support target setting.

For summative assessment, the criterion-referenced end of Key Stages or End-of-Year optional tests provided by the Qualifications and Curriculum Authority are used.

Sometimes, commercially produced tests are used. In most cases, the data collected are not of immediate use to the teacher. This is different from the use one makes of the day-to-day assessment data on children's learning, which is referred to as formative assessment. The following section offers some practical guidance.

Before considering the different ways we can collect information about children's mathematical learning, I invite the reader to try the following task. Write down all the ways in which you have made formative assessments of the mathematical learning of the children in your class. It is more than likely that most of you would say that you assess them all the time and it just occurs naturally. So what follows is an attempt to make you reflect on some elements of formative assessment which, based on research findings and my own experience, should enhance the formative assessment of the children you teach.

Factors which enhance formative assessment

As a starting point for this section let us consider what Black and William (1998b) consider to be the main strands in formative assessment. They are:

(1) The teacher developing the capacity of the student to recognise and appraise any gaps and leave to the student the responsibility for planning and carrying out any remedial action that may be needed.

(2) The teachers to take the responsibility themselves for generating the stimulus information and directing the activity which follows.

What follows should show how both the strands can in fact work together for the teacher to enhance the formative assessment system. So what are the elements that would contribute to the enhancement of effective formative assessment?

Effective questioning

The quality of our teaching is undoubtedly influenced by the type of questions we ask. As asking questions is an integral part of making assessments of children's learning, giving attention to the type of questions and how you ask them can often improve the quality of the information you collect. Concern for the quality of questions is raised by Black and William (1998b). They reported that many research studies showed the dominance of 'recall' questions and that the use of higher-order questions was infrequent.

In practice what does this mean? If you want to assess children's knowledge of facts you may ask questions such as:

- what number comes after 499?
- what is 56 + 10? or 9 × 9?
- what do you think these symbols are: %, + and − ?
- give me a list all the factors of 24.

These are *closed* questions, but their function here is to assess whether facts have been learnt. But if your intention is to explore the level of understanding of place-value or decimals it will require a more *open-ended* set of questions to enable you to probe into the child's level of understanding and any possible misconceptions. In the latter case, the type of questions you should ask may be:

- tell me why you think of …?
- what if …?
- that looks interesting, can you explain it to me …?
- would you rather work with fraction or decimals to solve this problem?
- which one do you think is the more elegant method out of these …?

The use of higher-order questions that encourage higher levels of thinking (described in more detail by Koshy 2001) should help teachers to get clearer insights into the quality of children's conceptual understanding. Although the use of closed and open-ended questions have their own place in mathematical assessment, a balance in the use of these types will ensure a better quality of assessment. A teacher will need to make a decision about the type of questions to ask and when to ask them. My experience shows that questions that assess recall and fluency may be asked during a mental starter, whereas questions that assess the quality of children's thinking will be required when observing children at work or during a plenary when children are asked to verbalise their methods of working out or their reasons for the choice of a particular method.

Using a systematic sampling record

Although most of the assessment is carried out during the daily lesson, there are occasions when a systematic observation format, introduced by Mitchell and Koshy (1995) as can be seen in Figure 8.4, may be useful. The task description is given in Figure 8.3.

In one of my action research schools, all children are assessed three times a year using a structured observation procedure. Linda, a Year 3 teacher, explained the rationale for the use of this procedure.

> *When we devised our assessment policy after a day's inset, we decided we wanted to carry out a structured observation of all children once a term. This is done by the class teacher with a focus group. Four or five children are observed during one session. The purpose is to have a snapshot of where the children are in mathematics at a particular time. We look for important aspects such as how children respond to investigations, their attitudes and any particular strengths or weaknesses which are not so easily detected during a busy daily lesson. The three tasks are varied – one per term – one may be based on place value, one may be an investigation and one may be a task which involves discussion and decision making. Nearly always, we find that teachers under-estimate children's capabilities or potential. This justifies our use of the sampling assessment sessions. The information we gather from this is of a superior quality.*

The formative assessment record reflects the true purpose of assessment and shows how the assessment cycle, teaching–learning–assessing actually works. The possible outcomes section lists the learning objectives of the activity. The teacher will observe what the children are doing and records in note form what the child does, says, the strategies used and make a note of any other significant indicators such as boredom, anxiety, persistence and so on. The data collected are then transferred onto the record and studied by the teacher or by a group of teachers (for moderation) and interpretations are made. Suggested action is also recorded. Action may vary according to the needs of the children. Linda explained that action

GRAB

A group activity – about 4 children.

Materials: A pile of cubes or pebbles.

Players each grab a handful of cubes or pebbles.

The scoring system is as follows:
2 points if you can make sets of 2 with no remainder.
3 points if you can make sets of 3 with no remainder.
4 points if you can make sets of 4 with no remainder.
5 points if you can make sets of 5 with no remainder.

That is the end of the game – each player totals his points.

With 8 cubes the game would look like this.

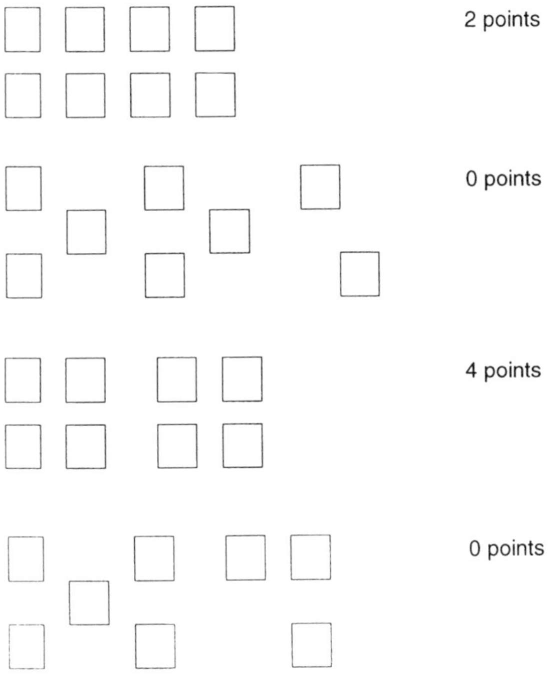

2 points

0 points

4 points

0 points

Total: 6 points

Figure 8.3   Task for close observation

could involve extra support lessons, recommendation to attend masterclasses or a possible interview with the teacher or the mathematics coordinator to explore any aspects of the child's mathematics learning or attitudes that may need further exploration.

A systematic observation procedure may be used for diagnostic purposes or for assessing higher ability so that appropriate action for individual help and support

```
╔══════════════════════════════════════════════════════════╗
║           Formative Teacher Assessment Record            ║
╚══════════════════════════════════════════════════════════╝
```

R ☐   Y1 ☐   Y2 ☐   Y3 ☑

Y4 ☐   Y5 ☐   Y6 ☐

Name: .....Anita...Stainton..................................... Date: ....

Activity: .....GRAB...

Possible Outcomes
• Counting (in groups ?) When handful is drawn, watch strategies
• Commutativity of multiplication and division.
• Times tables of x2, x3, x4, x5
• Idea of 'prime' numbers and vocabulary ?
• Addition of a string of numbers – strategies – mental?
Part(b) Discussion, working in a group, systematic work.

Account	Interpretation	Action
• Counted, in singles the first grab 24 and said :– 'you can share that into 2 and 3', then grouped into 4 and 5 to see if they work.	Not developed a good counting strategy – not attempted grouping.	Must show counting 'in groups' as more efficient to all children.
• Added scores accurately by writing as a 'sum'. Using fingers for bonds.	Commutativity Tables x2 x3, good recall – not x4, x5 Not yet fluent in calculations	Anita's target x4 , x5
• When 23 was obtained, said 'no, that will get no scores'	Awareness of 'Prime' numbers.	Use this context for a whole class discussion of 'Prime' numbers.
For Part (b) as with the other 2 in the group did not know where to start.	Lost!	The whole class – how to tackle investigation.

Comments: Part (b) was – if you could choose the 'best' number under 100, which one will it be ?

Figure 8.4   A formative assessment sampling record adapted from Mitchell and Koshy 1995

can be arranged. In Linda's school the evidence collected during the sampling sessions is shared with the parents and is also used for target setting.

Using the 'assess and review' sessions

The National Numeracy Strategy recommends that 'assess and review' lessons are built into the teaching programme. The use of these sessions is made clear in the in-service pack provided to schools (DfES 2001):

> *assess and review lessons are for assessing whether children have met key objectives. Teachers already know about the majority of children in the class from the dialogue and observations in earlier lessons. Assess and review lessons provide an opportunity for the teacher to focus on the few children they are unsure about.*   (p. 7)

In the light of the particular function of the 'assess and review' sessions, we need to consider three important factors that can make these sessions more effective. First is the choice of activity. The activity needs to provide opportunities for children to show whether they understand a set of learning objectives. It should provide just enough challenge for children to respond significantly. It should also provide opportunities for some discussion. Secondly, the teacher should prepare probing questions to ask (see Figure 8.5). Guidance is issued by the Numeracy Strategy in-service pack.

The third aspect is to consider the possible difficulties and misconceptions experienced by the children with a particular topic or concept. This will help to focus observation and collect relevant data in order to take appropriate action for individual children and for the whole class.

Providing feedback

An obvious point to make here is that the quality of feedback given to children is an important aspect of formative assessment. Since children's self-esteem plays an important role in maximising their achievement, this aspect needs very careful attention. As pointed out earlier, research has shown that there is a tendency for teachers to be guided by the quantity and presentation of work rather than focusing on the objectives of the lesson, when giving feedback.

Marking children's work is one of the ways in which children receive feedback from adults. As the main purpose of marking is to assess children's progress and to plan action, it is worth reflecting on some principles which will enhance the quality of the marking process. Marking should:

- be related to learning expectations – this means we need to focus marking on the learning objectives set out and understood by the children at the outset;

- use a variety of procedures to ensure the quality of feedback. Marking correct answers is only part of the process. Give credit to the use of sound strategies even when all the outcomes do not match the expectations;
- involve other adults who support the child in the learning process;
- provide sufficient praise and rewards for different levels of achievement;
- involve children in assessing their own work.

Year 3

Key objective:

Count on or back in tens and hundreds from any two- or three-digit number.

Probing questions

- *If you count in tens from 42, which digit changes?*

- *Why doesn't the ones (units) digit change? Show me on the 1–100 grid.*

- *If you start with 93 and count back in tens, what would be the smallest number you would reach on the 1–100 grid? Would 14 be one of the numbers you would say? Why not?*

- *What do you look for when finding a number one hundred less than (or one hundred more than) a given number?*

POSSIBLE DIFFICULTIES	NEXT STEPS
The children can count in tens (or hundreds) when starting from a multiple of ten (or hundred), but are less secure when starting from other numbers.	The children need more practice and may need to do more work based on the 1–100 grid (including filling in spaces on an incomplete or blank 1–100 grid). Use some oral and mental starters over the next few weeks. See page 13 of the Y1,2,3 supplement of examples. It may also be helpful to use a different resource, e.g. place value cards to show what changes when counting in tens, etc.
The children can count on in tens and hundreds, but have difficulty counting back.	As above.

Figure 8.5   Guidance of the use of probing questions for assessing mathematics learning

Self-assessment by pupil

Research studies (Black and William 1998a) highlight the fact that self- and peer assessment enhances formative assessment, which in turn raises achievement.

For Formative Assessment to be productive pupils should be trained in self-assessment so that they can understand the main purpose of their learning and thereby grasp what they need to achieve. (p. 10)

The authors maintain that the lack of this dimension of assessment being taken up is not because of the unreliability of children's assessment; in fact children are generally 'honest and reliable in assessing themselves and one another and, if anything, can be too hard on themselves'. The authors also suggest that the problem is mainly because pupils need to have a clear picture of which targets their learning is meant to attain. It is due to a passive learning mode that children find it difficult to assess their own learning. When teachers were asked about their perceptions and practices about children's self-assessment, in an informal survey of schools carried out by my colleague, most teachers admitted that they did not have a self-assessment system in operation, but the difficulty was explained in terms of lack of time. This state of affairs needs to be reflected on as self-assessment by pupils is an essential component of effective learning. Perhaps we need to consider introducing this aspect of formative assessment into our mathematics teaching.

In the context of mathematics teaching and learning, if organised effectively, there are two reasons for involving children in their own assessment. First, they will know what is expected of them as learners and, secondly, children will provide valuable insights into their own understanding through the process of assessing themselves. Although children will need training in these aspects, the impact it has on learning will justify the effort. It is not essential that a complicated system needs to be in place from the outset. There are different levels of self-assessment that children can employ. Checklists and smiley faces can be a start. These can then be developed into a more detailed semi-structured format as shown in Figure 8.6. I have found the introduction of mathematics journals to help children to become more reflective in the evaluation of their own work.

Achievement Record

This week we have learnt about the topic:

I think this topic is about:

A list of mathematical words and symbols I have learnt:

A list of mathematical facts I have learnt:

Make comments about how well you think you have learnt this topic and any other views you have:

Figure 8.6 Example of a semi-structured self-assessment format

Keeping portfolios

Most assessments of children's mathematical learning tend to be quantitatively carried out, using scores obtained by 'fill the blanks ...' or responses to written tests. Encouraging children to keep a portfolio of their best work is a step towards more effective self-assessment.

Black and William (1998b) declare:

> *A portfolio is a collection of a student's work, usually constructed by a selection from larger corpus and often presented with a reflective piece written by the students justifying the selection.*   (p. 45)

A 'child speak' set of assessment statements as in Figure 8.7 could become part of the child's portfolio.

Involving children to select their best pieces of work by judging against a list of criteria – these could include depth of understanding, level of competency, use of mathematical processes, elegance and fluency – would enable them to reflect on their own work and set their own targets. When I undertook research at the time of writing *Effective Teacher Assessment* (Mitchell and Koshy 1995), it was clear that children took great pride in collecting pieces of work for their portfolios. But it needed a great deal of effort on the part of the teachers to train children to evaluate their work before selecting their best efforts. At their best, portfolios can provide the following benefits to children's learning and assessment:

- they increase the motivation to learn;
- they give children some ownership of their own learning;
- they celebrate children's achievement;
- with some training children will learn to be self critical and reflect on their own learning;
- children will strive to do better than their previous attempt rather than compete with peers;
- they provide a basis for homework and parents evening discussions;
- the intrinsic satisfaction of constructing a record of achievement acts as a valuable reward and helps to develop self-esteem.

Construction of concept-maps and glossaries

How well a concept is understood can be assessed by asking pupils to construct concept-maps of ideas. A good concept-map will show how a child understands an idea and how that idea is connected to other ideas. For example, a concept-map of decimals may show connecting links to fractions and percentages. It may also show how decimals fit into the base ten numeration system. A multiplication

BURSTOW PRIMARY SCHOOL
NUMERACY TARGETS

YEAR 2

Name	Trying hard	Almost there	Success!	Teacher's initials and date
I can count forwards and backwards to 100 in ones and tens				
I can read the numbers up to 100 in words and numerals				
I can write the numbers up to 100 forming them properly				
I can count on in ones or tens starting from any two-digit number				
I can order numbers to 100				
I can recognise odd and even numbers to 30				
I know which part of a number tells me how many units there are and which part tells me how many tens				
I can count on or back in twos				
I can count on or back in fives				
I know all addition bonds for numbers 1 to 10				
I know all subtraction bonds for numbers 1 to 10				
I can add 9, 10 or 11 to a number				
I can add several numbers starting with the largest number or looking for number bonds				
I can add two two-digit numbers using a number line or 100 square				
I can subtract two two-digit numbers using a number line or 100 square				
I can double all numbers to 15				
I can double multiples of 10 to 50				
I can halve any even number to 30				
I can say the inverse calculation to 10 − 4 as 4 + 6 and state the other related facts				
I know the ten times table				
I know the two times table				
I can explain how I worked something out using words such as total, add and subtract…				
I can look for patterns in number sequences and continue them				
I know that I can use addition to help work out multiplication				
I know that multiplication can be done in any order				
I know when to add or subtract when solving a problem				
I know the ordinal numbers 1 to 20				
Any of the mental calculation strategies could be targets as well				
Level 2				

© Burstow Primary School
HM June 00

Figure 8.7 Self-assessment using 'child speak' assessment of objectives

concept-map may show its connections to equal addition and division. I have used concept-maps with our teacher training students and found that they can help to assess the level of understanding as well as any misconceptions and gaps. From a constructivist view of learning, which places children at the centre of learning as constructors of their own knowledge, it can be assumed that the more connections are made, the deeper a person's understanding of a concept.

Target setting

Target setting happens at different levels. Here I am focusing on setting targets for individual children. Target setting should follow many of the assessment procedures described in this chapter. Test results, day-to-day observation and listening, systematic sampling of children's work, self-assessment and portfolios can all be taken into account for target setting purposes. In the context of this chapter, the following general principles of target setting are worthy of consideration. Targets:

- should be set based on clearly explained learning objectives;
- should be related to assessment data;
- should be set in partnership with the child;
- should be expressed in language which children can understand;
- should be realistic and manageable;
- should set a 'just enough' challenge for the child;
- should explain what indicators of success are;
- should be monitored and revised regularly.

Summary

In this chapter, I have attempted to discuss aspects of assessing mathematical learning. In considering the purposes of assessment, my main emphasis was on the role of formative assessment in enhancing children's achievement. I have drawn on recent research findings on the role of formative assessment and, with the help of classroom examples, tried to provide a list of factors that should lead to effective teacher assessment.

References

Askew, M., Brown, M., Rhodes, V., William, D. and Johnson, D. (1997) *Raising Attainment in Numeracy*. Report of a project funded by Nuffield Foundation. London: Kings College.

Black, P. and William, D. (1998a) 'Assessment and Classroom Learning', in *Assessment in Education* 5(1).

Black, P. and William, D. (1998b) *Inside the Black Box: Raising Achievement through Classroom Assessment.* London: Kings College.

Black, P. and William, D. (1999) *Assessment for Learning: Beyond the Black Box.* Cambridge: University School of Education.

Cockcroft, W. H. (1982) *Mathematics Counts. Report of the Committee of inquiry into the Teaching of Mathematics in Schools.* London: HMSO.

DES (1987) *National Curriculum Task Group for Assessment and Testing.* London: HMSO.

DfEE (1999) *The Framework for Teaching Mathematics from Reception to Year 6.* London: Department for Education and Employment.

DfES (2001) *Using key objectives, National Curriculum level descriptions and National Optional tests at Key Stages 1, 2and 3 in mathematics.* Inservice pack DfES 0544/2001.

Ernest, P. (2000) 'Teaching and Learning Mathematics', in Koshy, V., Ernest, P. and Casey, R. (eds) *Mathematics for Primary Teachers.* London: Routledge.

HMI (1985) *Mathematics 5–16: Curriculum Matters 3.* London: HMSO.

Koshy, V. (2000) 'Children's Mistakes', in Koshy, V., Ernest, P. and Casey, R. (eds) *Mathematics for Primary Teachers.* London: Routledge.

Koshy, V. (2001) *Teaching Mathematics to Able Children.* London: David Fulton Publishers.

Mitchell, C. and Koshy, V. (1995) *Effective Teacher Assessment: Looking at Children's Learning.* London: Hodder and Stoughton.

Ofsted (2000) *Handbook for Inspecting Primary and Nursery Schools.* London: Office for Standards in Education.

Index